Praise for *It Is What You Make of It*

"In this amazing book, McRoberts does what all great artists do: he invites us into the transformation that he's been willing to do first. That transformation is the hard, vulnerable, and life-giving work of not letting things just be as they seemingly are, but performing the alchemy of turning it into creative gold. The journey of learning how to do this is essential, and McRoberts is the best of guides."

—SCOTT ERICKSON
AUTHOR OF *HONEST ADVENT: AWAKENING TO THE WONDER OF GOD-WITH-US THEN, HERE, AND NOW*

"Justin McRoberts is a consummate storyteller, and through story *It Is What You Make of It* imparts its gift—to remind us that we are made in the image of the Creator, that we are beloved works in progress with infinite opportunities to make more of what we have and who we are."

—CAMERON DEZEN HAMMON
AUTHOR OF *THIS IS MY BODY: A MEMOIR OF RELIGIOUS AND ROMANTIC OBSESSION*

"Throughout the years, Justin's words have deeply resonated with me, and this book is no exception. With humility and honesty, Justin opens our eyes to see the often forgotten truth: we are beloved children of God, created by a God who created us for more than we can imagine. Throughout these pages, we are beautifully reminded that our time on earth deeply matters, and this life is not for nothing but most certainly for something. If you're looking to be inspired and encouraged, this book is for you."

—TANNER OLSON
POET AND AUTHOR OF *I'M ALL*

"Most books on creativity are forgettable, and most books on purpose feel derivative. *It Is What You Make of It* is neither of those. Justin McRoberts has written an original, memorable book that will change the way you understand meaning and imagination. His stories and insights are more than regurgitated truisms; they are birthed from the experiences of a person who has spent years doing the hard work of actually creating. This book weaves together humor and advice, peppering each page with practical wisdom that any creative can incorporate into their own life rhythms. If you believe the world as it exists can be better and more beautiful—and if you feel called to help midwife that future—then you can't afford not to read this book."

—JONATHAN MERRITT
CONTRIBUTING WRITER FOR *THE ATLANTIC* AND AUTHOR OF *LEARNING TO SPEAK GOD FROM SCRATCH*

"Justin's real-life storytelling strips away all pretense and enables us to access a creative wisdom we all need. *It Is What You Make of It* hits you at the heart level and invites you to take an honest look at the motivations and inspirations that drive us forward."

—STEPHEN ROACH
HOST OF THE *MAKERS & MYSTICS* PODCAST AND THE BREATH & THE CLAY CREATIVE ARTS MOVEMENT

"With humility, humor, and hard-won hope, Justin invites us all to take an honest look at how our experiences (even the cringe-worthy ones) spark our creative spirits and shape our souls. *It Is What You Make of It* is like hanging out with a friend who manages to ask deep questions while making you laugh (and rethink some things) along the way."

—KAYLA CRAIG
AUTHOR OF *TO LIGHT THEIR WAY: A COLLECTION OF PRAYERS AND LITURGIES FOR PARENTS*; COFOUNDER AND HOST OF *UPSIDE DOWN PODCAST*

"Justin's ability to convincingly insist that there truly are no dead ends is both wondrously and painfully inspiring. It springs forth hope, even in the places I didn't want it to grow. Sometimes, to hope is to hurt, and *It Is What You Make of It* refuses me the permission to lay down my dreams and simply settle into what is. It calls me forward to keep reaching for what could be and to resist giving in to that sinister temptation that I am nothing more than a helpless victim in this dance called life. I think it will do the same for you."

—MIKE DONEHEY
SONGWRITER AND AUTHOR

"Justin McRoberts is one of the most prolific and gifted creators I know. *It Is What You Make of It* is a generous, heartfelt exploration of creativity, art, and the human experience. I was surprised by Justin's honesty in this book, and his clear desire to help us—to help me—become better artists and better human beings. Highly recommended."

—MATT MIKALATOS
AUTHOR OF *JOURNEY TO LOVE*

"I find myself audibly saying 'Yes!' to so much of Justin's work, and this book is no exception. *It Is What You Make of It* is a call to move beyond simply allowing life to just 'happen' to us. Justin invites us to ask the question, What are we willing to do to make our life an adventure of creation and cocreation? Each story will challenge you to ask, What if there is more? What if each failure and success is moving us beyond just saying 'it is what it is'—and into 'it will be what we make it'? This book is a memoir, a challenge, and a divine invitation."

—SARAH HEATH
SPEAKER, PASTOR, AUTHOR OF *WHAT'S YOUR STORY? SEEING YOUR LIFE THROUGH GOD'S EYES*, AND COHOST OF *THE MAKING SPACES* AND THE *ASK YOUR AUNTIES* PODCASTS

"*It Is What You Make of It* is a must-read for creators who feel stuck and uncertain of their next move. Justin McRoberts uses his familiar humor-filled tone to pull artists out of performance-based performance and into the understanding of transformational art (and life) making with and for others.

"If good art is hospitality (and it is), this book sets the table."

—JOY IKE

SINGER, SONGWRITER, CREATOR

IT IS WHAT YOU MAKE OF IT

IT IS WHAT YOU MAKE OF IT

Creating Something Great from What You've Been Given

JUSTIN MCROBERTS

W Publishing Group

An Imprint of Thomas Nelson

It Is What You Make of It

© 2021 Justin McRoberts

All rights reserved. No portion of this book may be reproduced, stored in a retrieval system, or transmitted in any form or by any means—electronic, mechanical, photocopy, recording, scanning, or other—except for brief quotations in critical reviews or articles, without the prior written permission of the publisher.

Published in Nashville, Tennessee, by W Publishing, an imprint of Thomas Nelson.

The author is represented by Alive Literary Agency, www.aliveliterary.com.

Thomas Nelson titles may be purchased in bulk for educational, business, fundraising, or sales promotional use. For information, please e-mail SpecialMarkets@ThomasNelson.com.

Unless otherwise noted, Scripture quotations are taken from the Holy Bible, New International Version®, NIV®. Copyright © 1973, 1978, 1984, 2011 by Biblica, Inc.® Used by permission of Zondervan. All rights reserved worldwide. www.zondervan.com. The "NIV" and "New International Version" are trademarks registered in the United States Patent and Trademark Office by Biblica, Inc.®

Scripture quotations marked KJV are taken from the King James Version. Public domain.

Scripture quotations marked NASB are from the New American Standard Bible® (NASB). Copyright © 1960, 1962, 1963, 1968, 1971, 1972, 1973, 1975, 1977, 1995 by The Lockman Foundation. Used by permission. www.Lockman.org

Scripture quotations marked NRSV are from the New Revised Standard Version Bible. Copyright © 1989 National Council of the Churches of Christ in the United States of America. Used by permission. All rights reserved worldwide.

Any internet addresses, phone numbers, or company or product information printed in this book are offered as a resource and are not intended in any way to be or to imply an endorsement by Thomas Nelson, nor does Thomas Nelson vouch for the existence, content, or services of these sites, phone numbers, companies, or products beyond the life of this book.

ISBN 978–7852–3988–8 (audiobook)
ISBN 978-0-7852-3981-9 (eBook)
ISBN 978-0-7852-3980-2 (TP)

Library of Congress Cataloging-in-Publication Data

Library of Congress Control Number: 2020952511

Printed in the United States of America

21 22 23 24 25 LSC 10 9 8 7 6 5 4 3 2 1

Contents

Introduction

The sculpture we call *David* didn't exist until Michelangelo took hammer and chisel and did the hard work of making it; up to that point there was only marble. Relatedly, Michelangelo had a hammer to use because, about 3.3 million years before he was born, some blessed sister or brother used a large rock to crush smaller rock into splinters and eventually strapped a stick of some sort to a similar rock and discovered they could crush rock with even greater force.

Just about nothing is what it is. Not in a world inhabited by people created in the image of God, in whose hands are both creation and resurrection. The capacity to make and remake is a thumbprint of the Divine on humanity. I'll go so far as to say that we dishonor our Creator when we give in to "it is what it is" thinking.

Love doesn't just win.

Mercy doesn't just triumph.

Light doesn't just cast out shadow.

Peace doesn't just get a chance.

Forgiveness doesn't just restore.

And time has never healed a single wound without the loving, attentive way people have spent that time after hurting one another.

All of these essential aspects of human life require the work of human hands—hands committed to a vision of the world made right (or at least a world made better). Hands of someone created in the image of God—which includes the ability to be creative. You were born with the capacity to create!

Maybe you weren't told that at home while growing up.

Or in school.

Or in the training you did for your job.

But if your teachers or trainers or neighbors drew a line between who you are and what you do (whatever it is), they were wrong.

Maybe you were told that you "just" teach

or you "just" parent

or you "just" coach

or you "just" lead your team at the office

or you "just" play your part on the team.

I'd like to help you see how limited is that view of who you are, what you're capable of, and maybe even what you've really been up to all this time.

The question in traditional art making is all about what to do with what we have on hand; it is a question almost always focused on what's next. For an artist, feeling "stuck" is just another call to creativity. "Writer's block," for example, is a way an artist's soul says, "This isn't the way I'm supposed to feel." The stuck writer doesn't say, "Welp. Looks like that's it! I'm not a writer anymore now that I feel stuck." She says, "I've got this problem right now. I'll call it 'writer's block.' I need to find a way to fix it or get out of it so I can get back to being who I am and doing what I'm designed to do; I'm a writer, after all." There are no dead ends for artists. Dead ends are simply more radical and challenging invitations to create a way forward.

And I get it; there is a virtual army of contentious voices around you screaming that life "is what it is," and particularly in places you feel stuck.

Your work life: "It is what it is."

Your social life: "It is what it is."

Your physical health: "It is what it is."

I'm saying that's all garbage. Your life is not just a set of stale circumstances that "are what they are" without any hope of change or improvement or transformation.

I don't know exactly where that voice is coming from in your particular life, but I want to help you locate it and shut it up forever. I'd like to help you silence it and replace it with something more like this:

> *I am a beloved child of God—the same God who created all things out of nothing. I am created in the image of that loving, creating, death-defying, circumstance-transforming God. I am a creature who creates. And anything and everything I do with my time on this earth and in this body is a reflection and expression of who I am.*

So I am going to tell you a few stories in expectation that, after reading them, you will look at your own life and circumstances and resources and opportunities and obstacles, step over that whole "it is what it is" nonsense, turn your eyes upward to the God who made you to be a maker, and say, "Let's see what we can make of this."

Throughout this book, I'll walk through key moments from my twenty-plus years as an artist, church planter, pastor, songwriter, author, neighbor, husband, and father, passing on lessons and practices I've learned about making something good from what I've been given rather than simply accepting it as it is.

I will invite you to see yourself as an agent of love and

redemption in your household, in your neighborhood, in your workplace, and wherever you find yourself. I will challenge us to wisely reexamine the apparently immovable systems you and I participate in (political, religious, economic) and to see our essential role in long-term change. I will invite you to believe that you are a partner with God in the renewing of all things.

"Christ in you," wrote the apostle Paul, "the hope of glory" (Colossians 1:27).

"Christ"—who took things like bread and dirt and water and made miracles—"in you, the hope of glory."

"Christ"—who took a small group of souls and built the global movement we call the church—"in you, the hope of glory."

"Christ"—who took death itself into his outstretched hands and made from it Life Eternal—"in you, the hope of glory."

Each of these stories is propelled by a constant prayer that sounds something like this:

"Let there be not one square inch in all of human existence about which you and I say, 'It is what it is.' Instead, may it be so that every moment of our collective time here together is marked by the power and potential of the knowledge that *it is what we make of it*."

ONE

Mr. Ross Sets the Tone

I went to Clayton Valley High School in Concord, California. I wasn't a great student until my senior year. Some of that was because I didn't like math. The larger part of it was that I didn't know what to make of high school. I had no intention of doing any of the jobs high school (as I understood it) was going to prepare me for. So I felt stuck and unmotivated.

Until I got in trouble in Mr. Ross's speech class. After that, everything started to come into focus.

Mr. Ross turned from the chalkboard and barked, "Mr. McRoberts!"

I stopped, mid joke, busted again for mouthing off in class. And this was speech class, no less. I mean, who gets in trouble for talking in a class about talking? Turns out Mr. McRoberts does!

I started packing up for a trip to the principal's office. That's how these things normally went for me: one joke too many and then *poof*—detention. But as I stood to leave, Mr. Ross stopped me and beckoned toward the front of the class.

"You can set your bag down." He walked from his desk to a closet door I'd seen him open maybe twice the entire semester. After rummaging around in the closet for a while, he pulled from it a large inflatable cactus and turned back to me.

Now, it's probably worth asking why Mr. Ross had an inflatable cactus in his supply closet. To the best of my recollection, that cactus had never made an appearance prior to that moment, and I don't think we ever saw it again. Which is to say, I haven't the foggiest idea why Mr. Ross had an inflatable cactus at the ready. But boy am I glad he did. My life was never the same afterward.

He led me to the center of the stage area at the front of the class and set the cactus next to me. Then, Mr. Ross took a seat at my desk and said, "Go ahead." I glanced back and forth between the cactus, which was almost my height, and Mr. Ross. The room buzzed with whispers and giggles. I was starting to feel off-balance and dizzy.

"What do you want me to do?"

Mr. Ross leaned back in my chair and said, "The floor is yours, Mr. McRoberts! Make us laugh. I will give you extra credit for using the cactus."

I don't recall how much time passed while I stood there with that silly plastic prop, feeling ridiculous and doing absolutely nothing. What I *do* remember (and will never forget) is that someone eventually broke the heavy silence, saying, "Sheesh, J. Just pretend you're in the desert or something! It's just a cactus!"

Mr. Ross immediately responded, "No. It's not *just* a cactus." He then turned to me, looked over the top of his glasses, and said, "It is what you make of it."

I'm guessing that, in one way or another at least once in your life, you have been handed an inflatable cactus of sorts and had no idea what the right or best next move was. Or you've looked around to find that, after all this time, nothing was what you thought it was and you weren't sure where to go from there.

Maybe it had to do with the job you can't win at but also can't quit. Maybe it had to do with the relationship that's been at the same dead end for months or even years, but you feel trapped in and incapable of fixing. Maybe it has to do with the passion project you no longer have the passion for but can't shake out of your head. Whatever it was or is, I'm guessing you know what I'm talking about. I'm also guessing that, along the way, you might have said something along the lines of "Welp, it is what it is."

And I get it.

That's a really convenient and comfortable thing to say: "It is what it is."

But lean in for a moment, and I'll tell you a secret.

I hate those words.

Actually, I hate them *a lot.*

I think those words are almost always a trap. I think those words are far too often a way to settle for less than what your soul wants, less than what your talents make you capable of, and *waaaaaay* less than what God wants for you.

I'd like to suggest that the power of potentiality is God's thumbprint on the ones made in God's image, and that it is *the primary* way to express the Divine spark at the center of human life. I might even go so far as to say that when I give in to "it is what it is" thinking, I dishonor the creative, redemptive, and loving God who made me and holds me together.

I've generally used the phrase "It is what it is" when I've come up against an undesirable circumstance or seemingly insurmountable problem. The issue I have isn't simply that saying "It is what it is" basically amounts to quitting, but also that the phrase is almost entirely untrue. Just about nothing in the realm of human experience simply "is what it is." Most every set of circumstances we find ourselves in is the cumulative result of decisions other people have made.

Admittedly, there's a *very* wide range of experience here. The dishes stacked up in and around the kitchen sink might be the direct result of a series of choices a spouse or roommate has made to eat without any plan to clean up afterward. That's pretty simple. Annoying as all get-out, but simple.

On the other hand, there are realities that are considerably more complex: like how nearly one in three human beings lacks access to clean drinking water.[1] Or that black Americans are nearly six times more likely to be arrested and imprisoned than their white American neighbors.[2]

Both of those realities have layers of complex causal histories. Regardless, none of those circumstantial realities was handed down from On High to simply be received and left unexamined, unquestioned, or unchanged. All of them can be changed. All of them *should* be changed. (Hold on for a moment while I go clean up the kitchen sink.)

Now, I get that a difficult conversation with a messy spouse or roommate sounds far less daunting than the deep, personal examination and work required to undo systemic racism and poverty. But at the heart of both movements is the question "What will I do with what I have on hand?"

If I respond to undesirable incidents or behavioral patterns (or even to evil itself) with "It is what it is," I relinquish my right and God-ordained responsibility to push back against darkness by adding my own light. Human history is not a sequence of cold, immovable circumstances begetting other equally cold, immovable circumstances with you and me either happily or unhappily in tow. Instead, human history is shaped by the ideas, the dreams, and ultimately the will and work of the women and men who actively create, tear down, reimagine, and rebuild. The undoing of evil and the making of good is and always will be a matter of will and work.

Until 1833, slavery was legal in the British Empire. Instead of saying, "It is what it is," William Wilberforce, British abolitionist, said, "Let's make it something else."

For the first 144 years of American history, women were not allowed to vote (even though they'd given birth to the *entire voting populace*). Settling for "It is what it is" just wasn't in the cards for Susan B. Anthony, Elizabeth Cady Stanton, and Alice Paul.

Even as I write this, nearly a quarter of the world's population lives in extreme poverty.[3] Many of those people are children who, because of their poverty, are far more susceptible to the exploitative practices of slave traders and pimps. I cannot, with good conscience, look at a world shaped that way and say, "It is what it is." Not even with something as seemingly monolithic as global poverty. Why? Because global poverty, far from being an inevitable and unchangeable circumstance into which certain people are born, is the ongoing result of a progressive series of choices made by those with power and influence.

I'm learning to intentionally look at what I've been given, including the more problematic parts of who I am, and instead of just saying, "I'm just this way" or "I am just the way I am," I'm asking myself, "What can I make of this?" The moments, stories, insights, and practices I've discovered along with my answers to that question are joyfully reshaping my life, and I hope your own answers reshape you, too, as you reapproach your life from a creative and redemptive frame of mind.

As you continue to read, I hope you'll notice how much I like to squeeze out every ounce of life in everything I do—including writing this book. And I'm not holding anything back here for one great reason: I think you're important. I really do. So is what you do at home and at work and in your community, as are the relationships you develop wherever you are. You're the only person in the specific combination of spaces and neighborhoods and networks your life binds together. Part of what that means is that, for better or worse, the choices you make and the patterns you set can and will *uniquely* change the world we share.

We all have to do our part, and what we make of the time, obstacles, and opportunities we are given is important. To put it a bit more grandly: I believe the creation of a more vital, just, and equitable world fundamentally depends on who we are, how we live, what we make, and even on

the images and messages we post,
the articles we share,
the stories we tell,
the books we write and publish,
the friendships we form (online and face-to-face),
the businesses we start,
the music we make,
the households we maintain,
the neighborhoods we enrich,
the families we cherish,
the marriages we build, and
the faith communities we shape.

It all matters.

Every inch of it.

The part you and I play in it is exclusively, blessedly ours.

Which means that because what you make from what you are given matters so much, so does who you are while you're making it.

Don't believe me yet? I get that. You may be used to the social narrative in which certain special people get to do influential and remarkable things while the rest of us stay quiet and out of the way, doing unremarkable and unimportant stuff because "it is what it is." But for the next few pages, I'm going to ask you to remember Mr. Ross. What was his thing? He was a public high school teacher with some weird stuff in his classroom closet and a loudmouthed wannabe comedian in the second row of his fourth-period speech class. Instead of saying, "Kids are disrespectful and self-interested and that's just the way it is," he asked, "What can I make of this moment for Mr. McRoberts?"

Thank God he asked.

Since then, it's been my turn to ask that same question.

Now it's yours.

What Do You Make of This?

At the end of each chapter, you'll find a section with this header. It will feature a few prompts, usually questions, to help you dig in a bit deeper or share your process with a few friends. This first "What Do You Make of This?" section will be a tad different. With this one, I want to help you get ready to use this book to change your life and world.

1. First, grab a journal or notebook. I'd love it to be a journal or notebook specifically used to capture and process what happens in you while you read this book and plan for what you'll do about it. If not, use what you've got on hand. If it's the same notebook you use to track meal plans and dinner recipes, that's fine. Just know I hate beets.
2. Now, take a few minutes to think about some ways you have given in to "it is what it is" thinking. What do you wish was different but don't think ever will be? What do you think *needs* to be different but don't have the hope it can be? Take your time and write it all down. Give your heart and mind a chance to sift through a few things that aren't as important to you so you can get to the bigger stuff.
3. When you feel you are finished, dog-ear that page or put a bookmark in it; we'll get back to it later. Just be sure that if there is a beet recipe in that same notebook, you put at least one blank page between the beets and me.

TWO

Frank Tate and Humble Beginnings

My career in music began the way so many others do: by moving into a house with a record label executive and being told I wasn't very good at music. It's the ole "boy meets record label executive, boy rents a room from record label executive, record label executive tells boy his music is garbage" story. It's an almost Shakespearian-level cliché.

Okay, that's not how it happens for most people, but it's how it happened for me. I was one of four single and nearly broke young men to move into Frank Tate's house that summer. None of us lives in his house anymore, but he lives in my head most days.

We weren't great housemates. Actually, we were pretty bad. Not only did we make a lot of noise, but we also made grilled cheese sandwiches directly on Frank's glass-top stove. Of course, we were helpful at times, too, like the time we facilitated the sale of Frank's furniture.

My roommate Chris and I were the only ones at the house when the doorbell rang.

"Hi, I'm here to pick up the armoire."

"The what?" I'd honestly never heard the word before.

"The armoire. It's the thing over there with the stereo system in it."

"Oh! Okay."

Chris helped me disassemble Frank's stereo, television, and speakers and then load the armoire, piece by piece, into the buyer's truck. As we did this, we kept muttering the word *armoire* under our breath. What a wonderful word for a piece of furniture! The stranger told us that his wife had read our ad on Craigslist and that he had driven right over to get this armoire. He handed us a wad of cash and drove off while we waved, happy to have contributed to someone's marriage while expanding our international vocabulary.

When Frank got home that evening, Chris handed him the cash and said, "This is for the armoire." I could tell he was really proud to have pronounced the word correctly and might have even thrown in a slight French accent for effect.

Frank looked at the cash and then back at us and then over my shoulder to the now empty space in his living room.

"What . . . ?"

As it turned out, Frank had never listed the armoire on Craigslist. He also wasn't familiar with the word *armoire*, and while we really enjoyed the opportunity to educate him on what we'd learned about the word and its history, that didn't make up for having sold his furniture without permission. It *also* turns out the piece of furniture we sold was worth about four times what the guy had given us. Fancy words = expensive stuff. Got it.

Side note: my favorite part of this story is that, somewhere later that day, that poor guy was trying to explain how he came home with the wrong *armoire*.

It's a marvel Frank didn't boot us from his place right there on the spot. It is even more of a marvel that, later that year, Frank would actually kick-start my career in the arts.

I had been writing songs as a kind of personal journal. Music wasn't something I had career designs for; my plan involved youth ministry and public education (the two places I was certain held the greatest earning potential). Songwriting wasn't a career hope; it was therapy.

Growing up, when I didn't know what was going on in my soul, I'd press Play and hope Tom Petty or Tom Waits or the Smiths or Rage Against the Machine might help me figure it out. They often did. Writing my own music was mostly an extension of that same practice, only a tad more intimate.

On occasion, I'd set up at a local coffee shop called Mocha Lisa's and play a few of the songs I'd written. Frank walked into one of those gigs at Mocha Lisa's and, as I recall, was there for all of two songs before disappearing out the front door. I remember feeling like it was pretty cool to have "the label guy" show up. Then, later that same week, Frank sat down with me on the floor in the empty space where his armoire had once been and asked, "Have you thought about playing music for a living?"

"No. You think I'm good enough?"

"Not at all. I think the songs are pretty bad, actually. But I like *you*, and I think you'll get better at the music part."

"Um . . . thanks . . . ?"

A few months later, I had a contract with 5 Minute Walk Records, and Frank brought me, as his featured artist, to a music-industry event in Nashville. At this event, radio people, store managers, and music buyers listened to live performances from the bands and musicians each label would feature in the year ahead. Most of the day saw a parade of bands or artists people were already familiar with who had shown up bearing gifts for the audience. While the room clapped and sang along with each artist, label executives handed out band shirts, hats, rubber bracelets, coffee mugs, and the like.

I was feeling more like an outsider than I could remember feeling anywhere previously in my adult life—a feeling exacerbated by the fact that Frank didn't bring a gift for anyone and that he opened up his introduction of me by pointing out that fact.

"I didn't bring you anything."

The room chuckled.

"I don't feel like I should have to bribe you to pay attention to us. If you like what we're doing, you should support us."

The room no longer chuckled.

Muted, nervous sounds sprinkled the room, mixed with the squeak of sweaty hands on new porcelain coffee mugs.

Then Frank gestured over his shoulder and said, "This is Justin McRoberts. He'll be our focus this year. I'll be completely honest with you—he's not very good right now."

I'm assuming my face wore the same look I saw on the other faces in the room—some combination of "Is he kidding?" "He has to be kidding!" and "Oh dear, he's not kidding."

Then Frank said a thing that (no exaggeration) reoriented my perspective on what it meant for me to grow as an artist and as a human being. "Here's what I'm counting on: Fifteen years from now, I think Justin will still be writing songs. I think those songs will be really good, if not great. I'm betting on the long term and inviting you to do that with me."

Then he walked off the stage, leaving me there with my guitar and a mic and my song. It wasn't good, and I knew it. But it didn't matter as much if I was good right then. It also didn't matter as much if I was bad right then. The moment didn't matter as a singular moment; it mattered as one in a long series of moments that would help shape me into who I was becoming. What mattered was Frank's commitment to me and my growth. I was in process. I wasn't just performing or achieving or trying to win. Not even close. Going into that morning, I knew I wasn't a great artist, and by the time I left, I knew it was okay to be "not great" and even "not very good right now"; it was more important to be devoted to the steps in my own development the way Frank was. He was thinking fifteen years down the line.

I would have expected someone in his position to not only hope for but *plan* for a faster-paced movement toward excellence and profitability. But only a few short months after that initial conversation in the empty spot where Frank's armoire used to be (and just weeks after he told the music industry I kinda sucked), I was on tour, opening for the best band on his label and playing songs off an album that was "not very good right now."

Along with being hopeful about the results of my long-term process, Frank was apparently okay with the actual steps themselves. Which makes me think of a story about Jesus.

Some folks had heard stories about him healing people, so they brought a friend, hoping Jesus would restore his eyesight. Jesus took the man by the hand and the whole group went for a walk, eventually ending up outside the Galilean village where they'd met. When they eventually got to the business at hand—the business of healing—Jesus apparently spit in the blind man's face. Now, while I'm sure this guy's friends didn't know exactly what to expect when they brought him to Jesus, I can pretty much guarantee they didn't imagine the process would involve anyone spitting in the man's face.

But that's not the part of this story that gives me pause every time I read it. The moment I trip over is when after Jesus rubbed the spit in his face, that man still couldn't see well; he wasn't fully healed. The way the writer of Mark put it, Jesus asked him, "Do you see anything?" and the man responded, "I see people; they look like trees walking around" (8:23–24).

I don't know all of what that means, to be honest. Maybe it says a lot about how bad off this guy's vision was or maybe it says something about the blind man's faith. I don't know. But what I can tell you about this moment is what bugs me about it. What bugs me is what might have gone through the heads of the people standing by, watching Jesus not quite heal someone. I wonder if, for a moment at least, they doubted Jesus was able to do the things they'd heard rumors about. In other words, it bugs me that Jesus might look bad. That even if what was really going on had to do with how bad that man's eyes were or that he lacked faith, Jesus would come off looking weak and ineffective. In short, I'm caught up on the optics. I'm thinking about the public-relations angle. Jesus, apparently, wasn't. And neither were the writers of the Gospels. See, I don't know what was going on in their heads or in Jesus' head because the writers didn't delve into those things. Thankfully, what I *do* know is that Jesus didn't get caught up in the moment the way I do. He didn't stop midprocess and concern himself with whether he looked like a failure; he stayed committed to the actual process and the actual people in that process.

Over the years I was with 5 Minute Walk (Frank's record label), my growth and development would cost

Frank. Getting behind a "not great" artist came with the risk of looking "not great" as a label, and he knew that from the start. But he didn't commit to only the end results of my process; he committed to my whole process. Frank flat out said, "This guy who isn't good at what he does is on my team." He publicly, emotionally, socially, and financially identified with me, saying, "Whatever happens in the next decade and a half with Justin and his music, you can put my name on it too."

That set me free to place less weight on each individual project, especially early on. Now, I still had to put the best I had at the time into each song or recording or performance. But that was the thing; I was only responsible to give the best I had *at the time*, so my art would reflect who I was *at the time* rather than reflect my whole career. Frank's vision and investment ensured that no single project, successful or not, would define me.

Whew!

That first record did well; more people bought it and liked it than we expected. Then, a year later, the second album didn't do as well as we hoped. When the numbers were up, I got to ask questions about what we had done to connect with people so well. I learned and grew. When numbers were down, we got to ask the same question from a different angle; what did we miss and how can we do better? I learned and I grew. And I think (actually, I know) that working with that posture and attitude is a large part of why there was a third album and then an EP and then a fourth album and so on. Believing I was a person and an artist in the process of becoming meant that there would eventually be over a dozen albums, a handful of EPs, countless blog entries, poems, sermons, seasons of podcast episodes, and a growing list of books, including this one.

Little to none of it would have happened had I thought I either peaked or bottomed out along the way. I didn't sit back and rest in any of my successes. And I didn't let any of my failures crush me.

I suppose you could say I have a career because Frank Tate spit in my face in front of a room full of people and then rubbed it in. And when I opened my eyes at first, success still looked like making money, and connection looked like sales numbers. Health still looked a bit like productivity, and people looked less like trees and more like opportunities to make something for myself. But Frank Tate stuck with the process and kept investing in me.

Eventually, success looked more like faithfulness, and connection looked like generous friendship. Health looked more like joy, and I now believe every person I've ever met is a beloved child of God, a sister or brother in their own process of becoming, someone who is worth eternally more than what I (or anyone else) can get out of them.

About a week before I finished writing this chapter, Frank called me to check in. Twenty-two years after he'd cast a fifteen-year vision for my life and work, he's still calling to see how things are going and if there are ways he can help. We talked for a long while about this book, and he kept saying, "Man, I'm so proud of you." Then, after I read a few pieces I was particularly happy with, he said, "Hey, I'd like to pick your brain. I'm finishing my own book and I'd like to run a few things by you. I love the way you tell stories, and I think you can help me."

We spent the next ninety minutes talking about what he had written (which is fantastic, BTW) and the small tweaks I might make if it were my project. Before he got off the phone, Frank said a thing that'll stick with me for the next fifteen years at least. "McRoberts, you're really good at what you do." And my mind buzzed with warm joy so loudly that I almost missed the next sentence. "Honestly, you're one of the best storytellers I've ever heard. Thank you for helping me with my book."

I hope you have friends like Frank. Not just people whose furniture you can sell without permission, but people who believe in who you are becoming, long-term—who believe it enough to invest and stay and celebrate along the way. I also hope you can *be* a friend like that to someone else.

(Note: if you're that guy who picked up the armoire that afternoon, I hope it worked out.)

What Do You Make of This?

1. Can you imagine what your life and work might look like fifteen years from now? What would you like to be true of you then professionally? Personally?
2. What current project or job are you concerned about possibly defining you? Or what past project or job is still defining you? What can you do to change the definition?
3. What hopes and dreams do you have for someone? Would you consider telling them about the potential you see in them, and the person you can imagine them becoming?

THREE

Missing LEGOs

My son and I didn't have it all together. Of the seventy-five pieces that made up the LEGO City Desert Rally Racer, we had only seventy-three.

At first we thought it was our fault. We figured that, in the few minutes since opening the box and emptying the plastic sleeves, we'd lost two bricks. So we spent the next few minutes crawling around on the floor with our faces pushed halfway into the carpet, scanning the terrain for anomalies. Then, we checked our pockets and the folds in our clothes. Nothing. Just in case, we checked the pockets and folds of clothes we had worn the day before. Nothing.

Asa (then six years old) boxed up the pieces we

did have, pushed his little hands into his pajama-pants pockets, and walked to the window to sulk. Because if you're going to sulk, doing it while staring out a window is the poetically correct way to go about it.

I poured a cup of water and handed it to him.

He took a long drink and said, "Now we'll never finish it."

I wish I would have said, "It's okay, pal. We can just log on to LEGO.com, navigate to the missing bricks page, describe the pieces we're missing, and have them delivered directly to our home!" You see, very occasionally LEGO will send out kits missing a brick or two. If you end up with one of those, you can fill out a form at the LEGO website, describe the pieces you're missing, and the LEGO people (presumably real people, but . . . maybe . . . LEGO people?!) will replace those bricks! Of course, I didn't know that at the time, so Asa and I just stuck with sulking for a while.

And as much as I mean to paint that picture comedically, I was also learning a bit of wisdom here: to give sadness and disappointment a moment when they show up. When I don't do that or when I just press on through sadness and disappointment, they tend to stick around and ruin better moments. When I give myself a moment to be sad and disappointed, I can *actually* move on.

So sulk we did. As I stared out the window, I thought about how much fun Asa and I had building together, which was really the whole point of doing it. I remembered that, most of the time, we weren't building from a kit; we were just grabbing pieces and assembling from scratch and memory and imagination. It also hit me that seventy-three out of seventy-five is 97 percent. (I definitely didn't do that math in my head, neither in the moment itself nor in writing about it—I used a calculator. #EnglishMajor.) That 97 percent is a better score than I ever got on anything during my entire scholastic career! We had a lot to work from.

I turned away from the window and started running my fingers through a pile of older LEGO pieces; some were from previously disassembled kits and some were just random bricks.

Asa knelt beside me. "What are you doing?"

"I'm gonna finish this thing."

He took one last sip of his water and started sifting through bricks with me. We found pieces that weren't perfect but just might work.

We tinkered
and built
and laughed
and disassembled
and talked

and planned

and tinkered

and built . . .

and when we were finished, it didn't look much at all like the picture on the box. In fact, a lot of the bricks that had originally come in the kit were still on the carpet, unused. We hadn't built the LEGO City Desert Rally Racer. We'd created the McRoberts Household Truck-ish Spaceship Thing. And it was perfect just as it was. Well, that's not true, actually. It was not at all perfect. It was something better than perfect; it was something we loved.

The French poet Voltaire popularized the proverb "Perfect [or more literally, 'the best'] is enemy of the good."[1] I originally found that an odd little saying, to be honest. That is, until I'd lived a little and tried to make a few things that mattered. Here's what I found out about Voltaire's quip: Anytime I started working on something, I made a truckload of assumptions about how it would end up looking or sounding or feeling when I was done. Then, as circumstances changed or other, newer ideas came into play, the project would veer off my expected course, and I'd begin to feel disappointment. That disappointment meant I couldn't accurately evaluate the benefits of a new idea or sound or direction; it was a "bad" idea because it wasn't in my original (and ostensibly "perfect") plan. Thing is, that "perfect" plan was never real. And that's true of pretty much every "perfect" thing: it's not real. Perfect things usually end up being inspiring thoughts that become an enemy of the good work I am *actually* doing.

Jesus originally asked twelve people to follow him. After Judas sold Jesus out, there were only eleven. That means, when Jesus left, they were stuck working with 92 percent of the original plan, and they were without an "instruction Emmanuel" (that might be the best/worst joke I've ever written). So how did his disciples decide who would fill Judas's place? They looked around at the group they had and got creative.

They asked who had been around the longest. That pared it down a bit. Then they asked, among those who'd been around, who'd seen Jesus after his resurrection. That pared it down even more. Eventually, they had two people left: Barsabbas and Matthias. But they couldn't decide between them.

So they cast lots.

That's pretty much like flipping a coin.

And on the strength of a fifty-fifty chance, Matthias became the new apostle. Why so casual? I mean, I know there was a bit of processing before the coin flip, but deciding who would fill in that rather delicate position by casting lots says a lot about the faith and posture of the disciples at the time. Which says a lot about what they'd seen of Jesus.

Not only did Jesus make some truly remarkable things happen, but he often did so by way of using whatever he had on hand.

"We're out of wine! What do we have? Dirty foot water?"

Boom! Party!

"This guy is blind. What do we have for that? Some dirt and spit?"

Boom! Vision!

"Seven thousand–plus hungry people! What do we have? Some kid's Doritos and a tuna sandwich?"

Boom! Another party!

I think I'd be missing at least part of the point if I read these accounts of Jesus' life and walked away with only the expectation that whenever I got into a pickle, God was supposed to come through with an out-of-the-blue magic trick and save the day. I'd be missing the part where Jesus first took notice of what he had on hand and decided it was plenty to work with.

In fact, in one of those accounts, Jesus looked over that massive crowd and then looked at the sack lunch a disciple had lifted off the one kid who brought a snack that day and said, "Thank God. We've got this."

Asa and I had seventy-three out of seventy-five

bricks, plus instructions. That's a lot to work with. More than enough. The disciples had eleven out of their original twelve, plus a history of watching and partnering with Jesus. That's a lot to work from too. What if, when things go sideways or fall apart, I give myself a moment to be sad and disappointed at what I've lost and then take the next moment to pay thankful attention to what I do have? What if that thankfulness is the fuel I'll need while creating what comes next? And what if that was God's plan all along?

See, I don't buy this whole idea of "getting out of the way so God can do God's thing." No verse in all the books of the Bible reads, "Christ, *once you're out of the way*, is the hope of glory." The one I'm familiar with reads, "Christ in you, the hope of glory."

You're part of that hope.

You share in that glory.

Your passion and innovation matter.

Your creativity and interests and desires and dreams count.

Which is why I believe that as you and I stumble . . .

and learn

and tinker

and build

and laugh

and disassemble

and talk
and plan
and tinker again
and build . . .

we are being shaped into people who make things that look as though God was involved rather than people who sit around expecting things to fall out of the sky, untouched by human hands. Sure, God's "fingerprints" are all over the thing, but so are yours and mine.

Don't get me wrong; like everyone else, I like the feeling of getting things right. The first time my son and I finished a LEGO kit together and it looked *exactly* like the picture, he and I were both on cloud nine (maybe even cloud ten). But—and this is a huge *but*—the McRoberts Household Truck-ish Spaceship Thing we created was something far more special than just one more kit that looks like the picture on the box. While it still looked like part of the LEGO world, it more reflected my son and me.

When we figured out we didn't have all the right pieces, we stopped trying to answer the question "How is this supposed to work?" and started asking "What can we make of this?" Both of those questions can be good. But sticking with one of these questions can get you stuck while the other can set you free. "How is this supposed to work?" isn't a bad question, per se. But sometimes it's just another way to ask "How do other people do it?" Again, that's a good question, but only for a while. Eventually, you find out that the people you think do it "right" made up the way they do things too! And now it's your turn.

There isn't a customer support page available for all of life's endeavors; you don't get to log on and describe the emotions and skills and partners you're lacking and have them delivered (potentially by LEGO people!) to your door. The question you're often faced with when things don't work out is this: What are *you* going to do with the time, talent, resources, and relationships you have on hand?

Let's be honest: it can be a sad moment to let go of your original vision.

The business that looks like that slick tech org you like.

The faith community that breaks the mold of the modern church.

The start-up that *Fast Company* will surely profile.

The bestselling book that turns into a movie and merch empire.

Maybe you'll need to go sulk out the window for a minute.

That's fine. Go do that. Just plan to return and dig back in.

How many projects or dreams or relationships are lying around your life in some form of disarray because you never took a moment to let yourself actually be disappointed and then, after a spell, got back up to see what you have on hand and started to tinker . . .

and build

and laugh

and disassemble

and talk

and plan

and tinker again

and build . . .

and eventually become the kind of person who makes the things you want to make—the kinds of things God created you to make?

What Do You Make of This?

1. What plan has gone sideways or maybe not even made it off the ground, and how can allowing disappointment, sadness, and frustration actually help you move on?
2. Once the dust settles and you've been able to grieve, what needs to happen next before you are able to take a realistic and thankful look at what you have on hand and start working from there?
3. What plans need to change, or what dream might have to die (at least in part), in order for you to change and become completely the person God designed you to be?

FOUR

Friends and Money and Starting Over

During the first few years of my career in music, my wife and I were on the road two or three months at a time. That made it nearly impossible to manage the online store we'd just put together. If someone bought something directly from me, they'd have to wait several days (if not weeks) for the CD or T-shirt or songbook they ordered to even be shipped. That's not a good turnaround time, even back when people used phones attached to the walls of their houses and the internet was "probably a fad." So a good friend of mine offered to manage the web store during my longer trips. He'd check the email account for order confirmations, let the buyers know their orders were being processed, package each order individually from the stock of T-shirts and CDs in my garage, and then ship them from the post office. He'd also keep up our supply of office essentials like packaging materials, printer ink, coffee, and so forth.

Having someone else run my store would mean not worrying that I'd automatically lose business to more streamlined online services like Amazon.com, which was a new and fascinating marketplace at the time. It also meant someone would have access to my house and garage, along with my bank account and a credit card. Having a friend on the job meant being safe from the kind of problems that might come from granting that kind of access to someone less trustworthy.

But that's not what happened.

My wife and I started to notice inconsistencies on our credit card bills. Which was a bit of a thing in and of itself since seeing those inconsistencies would require an art major and her English-major husband to do math above the number ten. But the trend was undeniable: higher-than-normal credit card bills, charges for items with odd codes instead of names, and a fair amount of things we didn't remember purchasing. Those inconsistencies over a few months added up to about $2,000.

I didn't want to come to the obvious conclusion. Instead I tried to imagine someone had cloned my credit card. Maybe even from a distance at a café somewhere. Something very spy-like. Maybe they had created a "from a distance" credit card cloning device they cooked up with gear from RadioShack! But the weight of what was clearly going on eventually broke that spell.

I called my friend.

He didn't answer.

I emailed him.

He didn't reply.

I reached out over and over but heard nothing back.

For days.

Then weeks.

Then months.

I didn't see or hear from this trusted friend for a few years.

I heard he was living in another town.

Then I heard he was on the street.

Then I heard he was in Thailand.

Every time I heard a new tidbit of information regarding my friend's whereabouts or doings, I'd chase it down. Over and over, I came up with nothing. And with each dead end, my anger grew. Eventually, I stopped wanting to work things out between us; I only wanted my money back. Well, that and I also wanted to hurt him somehow. I wanted vengeance. And the only thing worse than wanting vengeance is making a plan to get it. So, of course, that's what I did next!

I started calling his other friends and asking if they knew where he was. I'd tell them my side of our story and even, in many cases, tell them how much money he owed me, being sure to mention the exact dollar figure. Obviously, this wasn't a tactic designed to put things back together with someone I cared about; this was arson. I was willfully attempting to burn down his life.

Eventually, I followed the threads of a shaky rumor that he was back in town. That rumor led me to the door of his dad's place at 1:45 one morning, where I knocked loudly. The timing was part of my plan; it can be scary to hear someone bang on your door at that hour. The rest of my plan involved planting my hand on the door to keep him from closing it when he saw me, telling him to "keep his mouth closed," staring at him until I could tell he was uncomfortable, and finally launching into a very practiced tirade featuring words like *forthcoming* and *steadfast* and *jerk-face*.

But that's not what happened.

Before I could lift my hand to keep him from closing it, he opened it all the way. And I saw my friend standing there, not "the guy who owed me money." He and I had gone to the same church and had suffered through a lot of Oakland A's drama together. I knew his family. I knew his full name. I knew odd things like how many pairs of shoes he had. I knew the *person* in the doorway at 1:45 a.m., the life I'd been trying to torch because he'd hurt me. I knew him.

Recently, I've been struck by the way the writers of the Gospels talked about Judas. When I think of Judas, I usually think of the word *betrayal*. He's the betrayer. He's the bad guy. And not just in the gospel accounts. Judas is the bad guy folks often compare other bad guys to in order to establish how bad that bad guy is. He's *the* bad guy. But when Luke and Mark wrote about him, they identified him as more than just a betrayer. Certainly, when the disciples talked about Judas's history with them, they didn't shy away from his misdeeds and deceptions. But they also repeatedly referred to him as "one of them."

Here's Luke:

> Now the festival of Unleavened Bread, which is called the Passover, was near. The chief priests and the scribes were looking for a way to put Jesus to death, for they were afraid of the people.
>
> Then Satan entered into Judas called Iscariot, who was one of the twelve; he went away and conferred with the chief priests and officers of the

> temple police about how he might betray him to them. (22:1–4 NRSV)

And Mark:

> Immediately while He was still speaking, Judas, one of the twelve, came up accompanied by a crowd with swords and clubs, who were from the chief priests and the scribes and the elders. Now he who was betraying Him had given them a signal, saying, "Whomever I kiss, He is the one; seize Him and lead Him away under guard." (14:43–44 NASB)

It seems to me that, even after all Judas had done in betraying Jesus and the rest of the disciples, they still weren't willing to identify him as *only* "the betrayer." He wasn't just the guy who sold Jesus out; he was "one of the twelve."

Now, I have to imagine that as the stories about Jesus were being passed around and written down in those early years, Peter might have had a thing or two to say about what happened and how it was talked about. In fact, when the time came that the disciples decided to fill the space left by Judas, Peter stood up and said, "Brothers and sisters, the Scripture had to be fulfilled in which the Holy Spirit spoke long ago through David concerning Judas, who served as guide for those who arrested Jesus. He was one of our number and shared in our ministry" (Acts 1:16–17).

If you recall, Peter didn't exactly have the best record over that same stretch of time. Not only had he flat-out denied he even knew Jesus just a few nights prior to this scene in Acts 1, he'd tried to kill a guy with a sword in defense of Jesus. Not long before that, Jesus had told Peter that he'd be soon arrested and killed (a teaching Peter denied at the time, leading Jesus to call him "Satan," which is a thing that never happened for Judas, who also betrayed Jesus—and was "one of the twelve").

Maybe the only real difference between Peter and Judas is that Peter stuck around long enough to find out (and believe) that he wasn't just an accumulation of his mistakes; he wasn't defined by his wrongdoings. Peter found out that forgiveness was available to him. He got to become a new man.

I wanted that for my friend. I also needed it for myself. During the time my friend had been gone, I'd been a horrible friend as well, giving in to the sick desire to get revenge instead of the hope for reconnection and reconciliation. I hadn't shown up at the door that night/morning to act like Jesus; I'd shown up to act like a mob boss.

After a brief silence and before I could remember what the next step in my original, vengeful plan even was, my friend opened his mouth and started talking.

"Hey, man."

"Hey."

"I'm sorry."

"I know."

I don't remember all the details of the next hour, but I do know that by the time I was headed home, we had a whole new plan in place. He'd pay off the money in increments and, as often as possible, deliver each payment in person. That way we'd see each other and talk. Over time, the hope (the plan) was that we'd put things back together the way they were.

And again . . . that's not what happened.

We didn't get our friendship back. Not the way it was before. That's not usually the way things work when people hurt one another; we don't very often put things back together "the way things were." My friend and I weren't patching things up; we were forging something new from the pieces we still had. It was odd at times and uncomfortable at others. But that "new" friendship meant new kinds of risks and new kinds of adventures and new kinds of stories.

For instance, one early summer evening, I heard a soft knock at the door. I found one of my young neighbors (I think she was six at the time) standing there with her dad and holding an old photo album.

"Do you have a computer?"

"Yes, I do. Do you need to use it?"

"Can you help my dad find out how much he can get for these baseball cards?"

She went on translating her father's Spanish as he told me his car had been towed. Having moved to the East San Francisco Bay Area from Ecuador, he had misread a sign detailing the days and hours that parking was allowed on the street adjacent to our complex. At some point in the night or early morning, another neighbor had called to report the mis-parked car, and he was now trying to drum up enough money to get it back. Without his car he couldn't get to work, and losing that job would likely mean losing their place.

Stepping outside my doorway, I knelt and asked, "How much does he need?"

I don't know if you've ever had a car towed, but it can be an absolute nightmare. Not only does it mean having to figure out where your car ended up, but once it's impounded, the price for getting it out goes up rapidly. By the time they figured all the details, getting the car back was going to cost around eight hundred dollars. There wasn't a chance in the world they had eight hundred dollars in baseball cards on hand.

"I'll do some looking around, okay? Let's see what we can do."

They walked the one hundred feet or so back to their unit, and I went inside to make a phone call. I didn't even open my laptop because I knew I didn't have the baseball card knowledge to work it out. But my 1:45 a.m. friend did. I told him what was going on and how much money my neighbor was trying to put together. I sent him pictures of every page in that binder, and he did some digging around online for prices and places to sell.

"If we sold every card you've got, we'd probably get about fifty-five dollars."

I was deflated. If I'd gone back to them with that information, they'd have been deflated too. This could have been a really sad ending to this story.

But that's not what happened.

My friend took a short, deep breath and said, "You know what? Gimme a few minutes. I have an idea." About twelve minutes later, he called back and said, "I'll be over in a bit with the eight hundred dollars."

My jaw hit the floor.

"You said it was only fifty-five dollars in cards, though."

"Yeah . . . about that: you can give those cards back to your neighbor when you give him the money."

As it turns out, after my friend had hung up with me, he made a few calls to other friends and told them what was going on. He asked them to pitch in one hundred dollars per person to get my neighbor's car back.

"Tell your neighbor we all need second chances."

This friend and I didn't put our friendship back together the way it was before. We looked at the pieces of what had been our friendship at our feet and asked, "What can we make of this?"

The answer was "Something new."

That's the opportunity we most often have when things we build fall apart, particularly when those things are friendships; we get to forge new friendships that, like Jesus' body after his resurrection, are marked by scars from the past but aren't defined or debilitated by them.

What Do You Make of This?

1. What fault or failure of someone else's have you allowed to define the way you see them? What would it take to see them as more than their mistakes?
2. What fault or failure of yours have you allowed to define you? Did you hurt someone? Did you take advantage of them? Did you drop the ball and not come through the way you promised?
3. Did you lose a relationship or a project you just can't imagine putting back together? What happens if you start thinking of making something new from it? What could that look like? What parts of it are still worth building with?

FIVE

Everybody Hurts, Everybody Matters

In the fall of 2010, I started the largest and most time-consuming and energy-sucking creative project of my life up to that point (and, God willing, ever). I didn't know that when I started it. I just thought I'd throw together a few good ideas and have some fun! Then, I'd invite a small team of people to join with me, and the fun would be multiplied to party-like status. Only, this party was three people working way too many hours for nowhere near enough money, while I disintegrated into the worst version of myself anyone at the "party" could have imagined.

Cue Richard Wagner–oriented party playlist.

The project was a combination of letter writing and essays and music and lyrics and visual art and documentary-style video and stress and passive aggression and regular aggression and also personal reflections on relationships. Thematically, it was a celebration of community and a record of what my friends and family had made out of the circumstances and relationships God had gifted us. Eventually released in 2012 and called *The CMYK Project*, it turned out all right as a project. Sadly, it cost me a dear friend along the way.

One of the final phases of *The CMYK Project* involved the printing of a book. Actually, that's only partially true; it was two books. Actually, that's only partially true as well; it was really the same book in two formats. Somewhere in the process, we (and by "we" here, I mean "I") decided on printing two versions of the same book; one version was just a regular ole book with text on paper. The other was a two-hundred-page full-color extravaganza featuring artwork and photography and interviews (which I didn't mention in the description above, just like I didn't mention it to my team when we were working on it) along with letters and essays. It's probably also worth noting that we released the music on three separate EPs with three different covers and then selected a few songs from each of those EPs, rerecorded *those songs*, and tacked on *even more songs* to create a fourth musical aspect to the project—a full-length, full-band, studio-recorded album. So what we produced was . . .

a four-CD, twenty-five-song collection,

a text-only book,

a full-color book,

three physical art installations by different artists in different cities,

video interviews with each of the visual artists,

transcribed, printed versions of each of those interviews, and

the gradual, tragic disintegration of every relationship.

Yeah, yeah, yeah. I know . . .

It. Was. A. Lot.

The real fun begins with knowing that I'd never done anything like that before. In fact, I'd never made a book before, which was probably the most straightforward part of the entire project. To make that portion of the project simpler and easier on us (and by "us" here, I mostly mean "me"), my art director and I submitted the book-printing process to a large, reputable printing company. Having done what we thought was all the heavy lifting (writing, designing, formatting, arguing, walking away, and then returning to the same argument . . . blah, blah, blah), all that was left was to upload the book files; make the few, small adjustments we'd probably need to make; and then dance victoriously as the book (along with every other aspect of the project) found its way into the hands, hearts, and minds of readers.

Three days after the first upload, we got a notification that there were things in need of fixing. Like I said, we expected this, and while the list of corrections was quite a bit longer than we'd anticipated, we happily fixed the book and uploaded it again, thrilled to be done with this massively too-big and costly, and also ridiculous to the point of being beyond description, project.

Three days after that, the printer responded a second time with a list of errors, several of which we were certain we'd fixed. So I called the printer's customer service number . . . and I wasn't kind. Not even a little bit.

I was tired, and I felt that being tired somehow excused me from being kind. After feeling like I'd sufficiently communicated my frustration and disappointment, I hung up, and we dove into our third round of edits and fixes.

Then there was a fourth,

and then a fifth,

and a sixth,

and eventually, the same two things started happening every three to four days:

1. We received the same set of twenty-five notifications and necessary changes.
2. I ended up on the phone with customer service.

Over and over and over for weeks and weeks and weeks.

The only things that seemed to change were my level of frustration and the depth of insult I was therefore prepared to dole out over the phone to the agent I spoke to.

This went on for twelve rounds.

Quick math: twelve rounds times three business days per round (which means we're not counting weekends) means six-plus weeks, which, divided by seven days per week, factoring relational stress and a dwindling supply of bourbon = YIKES!!!

When that twelfth email came from the printer, I stared at my computer screen blankly until my art director spoke up. "I think I'll call this time, okay?" said Gary. "I'm not as angry as you are."

I left to run a few errands while he called the printer. When I got back, Gary told me he'd worked it all out. I wanted to know if "working it all out" meant he'd murdered anyone. He said no, which was slightly disappointing but probably for the best. What he meant by "working it all out" was that he'd asked to speak with a supervisor, just as I had. And just as had happened when

I'd called, Gary was told they didn't *have* supervisors. But then, instead of losing his cool and insulting the person on the other end of the call (my strategy), Gary calmly described our situation and history in detail and kindly but firmly asked who he should be talking to.

"You need a specialist," the agent told him.

In eleven previous calls, I'd never even heard the word *specialist* much less been given the option to speak to one.

Gary said he held the line and was connected to someone we will call, for the purposes of this story, "the Specialist." Gary described our situation, and the Specialist said she thought it was "really odd." Gary assured her he was aware of how odd it was and then asked what we needed to do. The Specialist asked Gary to upload the file again.

"With all due respect," Gary replied, "we've uploaded the file a dozen times now."

"I can see that," said the Specialist. "This time, I'll stay on the phone with you and wait for it to hit our system. Then we can look at the file together."

Ten minutes later, Gary and the Specialist were looking at the file together.

"Is your file supposed to be five by eight or six by nine?"

"It should be six by nine."

The Specialist paused and then asked Gary if she could call him back. Twenty minutes later, she called back and told Gary what was actually going on. It wasn't that their system had a glitch or that our file was corrupt or even that we were doing something technically wrong.

It was much worse and far weirder than any of that.

During one of the early phone calls in the editing process, I'd said something pretty horrible to one of the technicians. In turn, he'd reset the specs on our project from six by nine (which was correct) to five by eight, so that every time we uploaded the file, it would trigger dozens of warnings and be rejected. The technician had sabotaged our project. That's a pretty horrible thing to do to someone. But he did it because I'd been horrible to him.

Now here's what's really funny (and by "funny" I mean painfully ironic and related to my social ineptitude): the full title of *The CMYK Project*—the book plus three EPs plus full-length LP plus visual art plus video plus other book—was *CMYK: The Process of Life Together* and was promoted as "a celebration of life in relationship." It was chock-full of stories and anecdotes about getting along with and loving other people, particularly where there were differences of opinion and experience. It was a project about my own process of learning to love people the way Jesus loved people.

So . . .

Can you imagine being the tech on the other end of the phone, staring at a chapter about the unconditional love of God while the author of that chapter calls you names? Perhaps you'd think the love and kindness described in those pages weren't for you. And if I'm honest, I certainly wasn't offering them to that customer service agent, because in my mind he wasn't a person but an instrument. I talked to him the way I talk to the car that won't start or the software that freezes. His value was entirely predicated on how useful and helpful he was to me.

My encounter with that tech reminds me of one in the gospel of Mark: the one about a woman whose body was healed when she simply touched the clothes Jesus was wearing. It's a remarkable story in a lot of ways. First of all, that was quite an ensemble Jesus had on, right? I've got a few favorite shirts, but none of them have mystical healing properties. More significantly (and less jokingly), I am captivated by the choice Jesus made to stop and talk with the woman who touched "the hem of his garment" (Matthew 9:20 KJV). Because the way he handled the moment says far less about the clothes he had on or even his power to heal and far more about how important and valuable she was to him.

As the writer of Mark told it, a man named Jairus,

whose daughter was dying, went to find Jesus to ask for help. Jesus was up to other things at the time, but he changed course when Jairus asked him to heal his daughter. That part makes sense to me. Jairus led a synagogue, which made him a big deal in social, political, and religious circles. Helping Jairus presented a legitimate opportunity to heighten Jesus' profile, prove a few folks wrong, and "get the message out," as it were.

But as Jesus was following Jairus back to his home, the trajectory of the story changed.

> And a woman was there who had been subject to bleeding for twelve years. She had suffered a great deal under the care of many doctors and had spent all she had, yet instead of getting better she grew worse. When she heard about Jesus, she came up behind him in the crowd and touched his cloak, because she thought, "If I just touch his clothes, I will be healed." Immediately her bleeding stopped and she felt in her body that she was freed from her suffering." (Mark 5:25–29)

Jesus then asked about who touched him, which a few of his friends found a bit silly, seeing as though there was a whole mob of people jostling about and bumping into one another. But to Jesus (and this is the part that gets me), this woman wasn't just another person in the crowd. Which is why I absolutely *love* the way the writer of Luke wrote about this same story. As he retold it, when Jesus asked about who touched him, she tried to stay hidden but eventually conceded that "she could not go unnoticed" (Luke 8:47).

How good is that?

"She could not go unnoticed."

Jesus stopped, and along with him, the whole crowd that had been following him. I don't know how long their conversation went on, because none of the writers who captured this moment provided that detail. But apparently it was long enough for Jesus to hear a lot of this woman's story. She'd been sick and bleeding for twelve years with multiple medical failures along the way. The other thing the story makes clear is that Jesus was invested enough in the conversation that someone else had to interrupt him and let him know Jairus's daughter had died.

Now, it's significant that once Jesus finally did arrive, he assured the people in Jairus's household that, despite appearances, he had things in hand and could still heal Jairus's young daughter. That says to me that Jesus had enough confidence in his ability to do the work he'd committed to that he could pause for a moment along the way and turn his full attention to a person he'd met so that "she didn't go unnoticed."

That customer service agent wasn't just another

person along the way, though I treated him like he was. Since *The CMYK Project*, I've learned that . . .

the customer service agent helping me sort out font problems during manufacturing,

the Apple Genius Bar employee helping restore my lost data,

my web developer,

the barista or bartender serving me while I write,

the UPS or FedEx driver delivering proofs,

the neighbor whose dog pops over to play ball while I'm editing,

the dog herself who wants to play ball . . .

all these people are *actually* people (except the dog, who is not a person but thinks she is, so we'll keep her on the list). They are, each of them, beloved ones of God with dreams and hopes and problems and opportunities and relationships and needs and gifts and strengths. They are the kinds of people worth making great work for. Which also makes them the kinds of people worth *stopping* great work for, whether or not they're directly part of that work process or not.

They aren't stepping-stones on my path to success.

They aren't cogs in the wheel of my productivity.

They aren't part of my "system."

Even (and especially) if they're part of my team working to complete a project.

Remember a moment ago when I asked you to imagine being the technician on the other end of the phone, staring at an entry about the unconditional love of God while the author of that page yells at you and calls you names? Well, let's take that one step further, shall we? Because that's where the deeper learning lesson was for me.

Imagine being my art director, Gary, who took on that final phone call to put the project back on track after I'd derailed it with my anger. Imagine working for nearly two years on a project ostensibly celebrating the unifying love of God for people while watching your partner and project leader verbally abuse customer service agents over the phone and then carry that anger around the office every day. Maybe you'd lose respect for that person. Maybe you'd have a hard time trusting them as a leader or a friend. Maybe you might even decide that was the last time you'd work with that person or anyone like them if it meant being treated that way or being party to treating others that way.

You see, what I know now is that how I treat the people I work with . . . nope. Let me fix that:

What I know now is that how I *love* the people I work with and for and around says ten thousand times more about who I am than any project or job or end result, regardless of its effectiveness, beauty, impact, or market success. I'd rather make garbage work while honoring and maintaining great relationships than create bestselling work while becoming the kind of person nobody wants to be around.

It was and is the love in Jesus that was and is the source of healing, whether on the street, in a crowd, or in the back room of a powerful social figure—which is to say, Jesus was the same person wherever he went.

I want to live like that.

I want that kind of love to dictate the way I work.

The way I'd addressed the young man at the printing agency had almost nothing to do with his job or position or the fact that I didn't personally know him; it had everything to do with me and my character. Yes, the professional distance between us made it easier for me to be unkind, but the capacity to dehumanize someone and use them for my own purposes was in me from the start. And here is something true: I don't get to (and shouldn't want to) make anything out of someone else's life. That's not my job. My vision isn't big enough for your life. That's God's job. Only divine hands can make something out of a human life without belittling, stifling, and minimizing that person in the process.

About four years after that first book came out, my third book hit the shelves. It was a book of prayers I'd collected from my own practice, born out of trying to live more intentionally. Among them was the prayer I wrote shortly after the completion of *The CMYK Project*. It reads,

> May the work I do
> never become more important to me
> than the people I get to work with
> or those I'm working for.

What Do You Make of This?

1. When have you felt used by someone? What was that like? How did you handle it?
2. What people in your "system" have you overlooked regularly? How can you change that?
3. When you think about your legacy and what you'll leave behind, do you think more about projects to accomplish than the people you work alongside? What will it take to make the shift to valuing people over projects?

SIX

They're Not Here to See You Fail

I used to see the band Primus every year on New Year's Eve. I don't know how many years in a row I did that, but it was a lot of years, and I know that because I remember seeing a good number of opening acts: the Melvins, the Charlie Hunter Trio, Mr. Bungle, and a few others. Because of the connection Primus had with their audience, those opening acts were generally well received, even if they weren't very well known. That is, until the year Primus invited the band Cracker to open for their NYE show. That didn't go so well.

Cracker was more traditionally popular than any

band I'd seen open for Primus on New Year's Eve. They'd released a few strong singles that year, including "Low," which climbed onto the Billboard Top 100 singles. None of the other bands I'd seen open for Primus had ever had a top 100 single. In fact, I don't think Primus themselves ever had a top 100 single. So, for a lot of Primus fans, including me, it was a bit odd to have this major-market success open for the street-level band we knew and loved. I'm only telling you this because I'm about to share how numerical success and market popularity can be really bad replacements for the kind of connection that makes work of any kind great.

Cracker opened their set with "Low," and just about everyone in the place knew the song. Thing was, as the crowd sang along, it wasn't with a spirit of camaraderie; it was in a clearly mocking tone that said, "Yeah, we know this song because it's popular, and because it's popular, that makes us not like it, so we are going to sing it *at* you instead of *with* you, and also, neener, neener."

The band picked up on the tone of the nearly five thousand people jeering and mock-singing along. They took what seemed like an intentionally long time tuning their instruments between "Low" and their next song. As front man David Lowery started toying with the crowd, whatever he was saying was quickly drowned out by a crescendo of boos and insults—and bottles of water and beer tossed at the stage.

That's when Cracker started in on their second most popular song, "Euro-Trash Girl." It is worth noting at this point that the song was recorded in two versions. One of them, the radio single, was pretty long for a radio single, clocking in at just under five minutes. Then there was the album version, which was over eight minutes long. Now, an additional three minutes is not that long, but it seems like an eternity when you're waiting for the opening act to finish so you can hear the headliner you care about. Which is why I'm certain the band opted for the eight-minute version, featuring three different guitar solos and regular intervals of comical, lyrical jabs from Lowery.

I'd never seen anything like it before.

I've never seen anything like it since.

That's because it's rare.

Very rare.

No normal person shows up wanting to see someone fail, even in sports—unless you someday want to experience Yankee Stadium but can't stand the Yankees. As fans and supporters and consumers and friends, we want to see you win. I don't go to restaurants hoping the food is foul. I won't go to a movie I hope disappoints me (unless I'm a Star Wars fan, which is an *entirely* different thing). And I don't go to concerts hoping the band is bad at music. If I'm going to spend my time and energy and money to see you do your thing, I'm hoping, for my sake *and* yours, that you crush it!

As much sense as that makes on one side of that relationship (fans and supporters and consumers and friends), it's *amazing* how hard it is to believe on the other side of it (makers, bosses, creators, moms, dads, performers, and anyone involved with anything Star Wars–related).

Years after seeing Cracker open for Primus, I got to see the first public performance by a young woman named Ethel. Ethel is not this person's real name. I don't remember her real name because I'm bad at names. I definitely wrote it down (on a napkin, I think) because I told her that the story I'd just witnessed was worth passing on and that I'd eventually write about it in a book.

I lost the napkin with Ethel's name on it.

Or maybe it was Bethany . . . ?

I don't recall.

What I do remember is that, as part of a local nonprofit's annual fundraiser, Ethel was asked to play a song. The nonprofit focused its work on teenaged women, and she was a teenaged woman who had been affected by its work. She had written a song about her journey with the program, and her song was scheduled for the time slot immediately following the keynote speaker. Music to write checks to, as it were.

My wife and I arrived early to help set up for the event. Mostly, we rolled tables into position and set up eight chairs per table. As we rolled our tenth table into place, I spotted Ethel fumbling around with her guitar and mic. She had two song sheets that kept fluttering off the music stand next to her as she shakily adjusted and readjusted the mic and music stand. Amy pulled the table we were rolling out of my hands and said, "Hey, you should see if you can help her."

I wasn't entirely sure how to start that conversation since "Hey, you look like an emotional wreck, can I help you?" felt like a bad lead-in. Then I saw her digging around her pockets and guitar case the way I do when I don't have a guitar pick. That presented the perfect window of opportunity. See, I generally have a pocket full of guitar picks. It's a habit, I guess. Some people carry around a lighter or gum or an answer for everything. I have guitar picks. Even these days when I play only a handful of shows a year, I'll still have ten or twenty orange Tortex .60 mm picks in my right pocket. Certain days, it's the way I know which pants are today's pants.

I approached the stage and offered Ethel a few orange picks. She took them without saying anything, which I knew wasn't because she was being rude. She was really nervous; her hand was trembling and her breaths were far too shallow and frequent.

"So what are you going to play tonight?"

"I dunno. I was gonna play this one song, but . . . I dunno."

"Yeah, no, yeah. What's the name of the song?"

"You wouldn't know it. I wrote it myself."

"Ah. That's super cool. So if you don't do that song, what else would you play?"

"I only have one song."

"Oh . . . well." I contorted my face to look like that emoji with the nervous eyes and clenched teeth. The "yikes" emoji. She looked up and giggled, which turned into a laugh, which meant I could share in it.

"I'm sorry. I'm just nervous. I don't want to embarrass myself. I don't want them to hate me."

Now, there's probably some significant psychological insight here about projecting one's own fears onto other people. I don't honestly know how any of that works. What I *do* know is that, in nearly a quarter century of stage work, I've just about never met a room of people who had shown up to see me blow it so they could hate me.

I mean, don't get me wrong—I've definitely been ill-received at times.

I've had batteries thrown at me.

And marshmallows.

And money! (Boy, that's a good story for another book.)

And yes, there's that story about Cracker opening for Primus. But that's why I told you about it before we got to the part about Ethel. Nobody was going to show up that night thinking, *I can't wait to see that young woman bomb! I'll save my dessert for after.* Real adult life isn't a fail-video compilation. Beloved, *nobody* is watching you in the hopes that you'll fall on your face and injure yourself. Everyone you know hopes you'll make it.

Everyone in the room wanted Ethel to do well, including the event's organizers. They'd invited her to perform at this fundraiser because they liked and valued the song she'd written and thought it was a good enough representation of *their* work to make it part of the fundraiser. And they needed the fundraiser to go well so they could keep doing what they wanted to do.

I did my best to tell her all that without making it feel like pressure. Eventually, she took a long, deep breath and said, "I guess it's all the people I don't know."

So I asked her if she knew anyone in the room.

"My sister and a few friends are here."

She pointed at them and they waved.

And then giggled.

And then waved again.

"Have they heard you sing before?"

"Oh, yeah. I play them things all the time."

"Okay, then. Before you start, be sure you know where they are in the room. Then, when you feel nervous, look at them and trust what you see on their faces. They like you and they like your music and they're proud of you."

She killed it. And I mean "killed" in the good way, not the "mob boss found you annoying and inconvenient" way. I also don't mean she was flawless. She actually forgot a lyric in the second verse of her own song. When she did, my heart sank for a moment. I thought I'd given her the guitar pick she'd frame and point to while she told her grandkids why public performance was "the devil's work." But instead of giving in to nervousness and quitting, she looked up and found her sister and her friends, two tables from the stage.

She nodded.

They waved.

And then giggled.

And then waved again.

Then she took a long, deep breath and laughed at herself, which got everyone in the room laughing, including me. When she jumped back into the song, she had more energy, more confidence, and a far clearer singing voice than before. Five minutes later, I was on my feet, clapping and cheering, right along with everyone else in the room.

She'd won.

Just like we hoped she would when we showed up.

And so will pretty much everyone who shows up for you.

Take a moment to think about concerts or movies or shows or podcasts you pay attention to. How many of them are you hoping are trash? I'm guessing none of them. Let's take that a step further: Have you ever seen your favorite band on an off night? Do you remember the worst episode of your favorite TV show? Can you think of the worst part of your best friend's or spouse's personality? Do you remember thinking, "There it is! The moment I've been waiting for through all these better moments!"? No, you definitely didn't think that.

And neither will pretty much anybody who shows up for you.

Because pretty much nobody shows up to see people fail. People show up because they want to see you win.

According to the ancients who wrote the Old Testament, when God created the world we live in, he then handed the keys to someone like you or me or Ethel. Or even Cracker's lead vocalist, David Lowery. And I have to believe that God's hope and intention wasn't "I can't wait until this loser blows it so I can fix it." I think God hoped and intended and planned to see you and me flourish and then made accommodations (dramatic, costly, and destiny-altering ones) for even the most complete of our failures, so that when we did blow it, we could still flourish if we showed up, set our song sheets on the music stand, and gave it our best effort.

What Do You Make of This?

1. Where or when have you blown it professionally? How did you move forward from that moment? Or why are you holding on to that memory like some weird trophy?
2. Who on your team is going to be there no matter what? How can you ensure they're witness to what you're doing now? And how can you ensure they are witnesses to what you do next?
3. Who around you is afraid of their own failure? How can you help them? What do you have in your pocket that might open the door to solidarity?

SEVEN

KISS Army and Becoming Something Beautiful

The glam-metal band KISS wrapped up their legendary "Dynasty" tour on December 16, 1979. Roughly five months later in Concord, California, was what I believe to be the first (and likely only) KISS tribute show featuring a six-year-old onstage.

Yes, I was that six-year-old. And, yes, there *are* pictures.

One of the many benefits to growing up in my neighborhood was being surrounded by older kids who not only had a far deeper appreciation for music and wider range of musical taste but also had stereo systems. Chris Livermore's Kenwood system seemed to me a thing delivered directly from the future. The stereo tied into his Technics SB-A50 speakers, which stood about my height at the time, so we didn't just hear the music; we were drawn *into* the music. Most of the time, I heard music played through the small, tinny speakers of my mom's Toyota Corolla. But in Chris's room, the volume and quality of his system meant being enveloped by the sound.

I would sit with my back against Chris's bedroom wall, sometimes with a few other kids from the neighborhood, while Chris introduced us to R.E.M., U2, Rush, Huey Lewis, Run-DMC, and many others. It was because of those magical listening sessions that my second-ever album purchase was *Synchronicity* by the Police, a rather savvy and mature album purchase for an eight-year-old. Of course, it's probably worth noting that the album I purchased before that was *Chipmunk Punk* by the Chipmunks. My taste was eclectic.

But before the Police, and even before the Chipmunks, there was KISS with all their

hairspray,
face paint,
leather and armor and platform boots,
and rock songs, mostly about girls.

Chris was a member of the band's fan club, KISS

Army. Being in the Army came with perks like the option to order each new KISS release through the mail and have it delivered to your house. On the day *Dynasty* showed up in our neighborhood, we sat motionless on the floor of Chris's room, listening to this gift from the heavens (via Casablanca Records and delivered by the USPS). For long minutes, the only movement in that room was Chris getting up to flip the record over and setting the needle on side B . . .

. . . then again to start side A over . . .

. . . and then side B yet again.

Over the next two weeks or so, we listened to the album over and over until we knew every guitar solo, every drumroll, and every word (even the "bad" ones). But even *that* level of musical immersion wasn't enough. We wanted to inhabit that album; we wanted to *be* KISS. So, as the oldest among us and the only official member of KISS Army, Chris hatched a plan.

He cut holes in our shirts and tore the sleeves off. He twisted aluminum foil into links and wove it into chains. He collected emergency flares from his parents' cars. (More on this later.) When Chris realized how little he knew about makeup, he enlisted the help of his sister. In exchange for Heather's help, she asked to be part of the band.

As it turns out, that was very helpful. KISS had

four members, and there were only three of us to that point: Chris was Paul Stanley, Kai was Ace Frehley, and I was Gene Simmons. *Nobody* wanted to be Peter Criss, because nobody wanted to wear the cat-whisker makeup. Thank you, Heather. Also, I'm so sorry you had to be Peter Criss.

Parents, siblings, and neighbors gathered around the wooden play structure in Chris's backyard to watch (in what I can only assume was a mixture of confusion, amusement, fear, and good humor) as we took the "stage" in our torn shirts and wrapped in aluminum chains. We put the needle on the record and struck our best rock-and-roll poses, and for just shy of twenty minutes, we strummed our cardboard instruments and lit the emergency flares we'd jammed into the ground around our feet. We stopped just long enough for Chris to turn the vinyl over and drop the needle on Side B. Then, for nineteen more glorious minutes, we were once again our favorite band in the world; we were Kid KISS.

Sometimes we talk about inspiration as if it simply happens, as if it just shows up when it wants to and leaves as quickly. I don't think that's true. I think, in the moments when we recognize we are captured by something, we have an opportunity to practice that inspiration, to make something of it. Maybe more poignantly, we have the opportunity to be made into something or become more fully who we already are.

My friend Sara tells a story about her first encounter with the work done by International Justice Mission (IJM). There are millions of people around the world currently living in some form of slavery, and not enough people are doing enough to get them out or to shut down the operations that facilitate such injustice. IJM is one organization that is attacking this problem, and as a supporter, I am regularly inspired by what they do.

As Sara tells it, she had been invited to an event designed to highlight IJM's history, vision, and work. I've been to a few of the events they put on, and everything about them is top-notch. Sara was moved by what she saw and heard, so she set up an appointment with IJM's founder, Gary Haugen. Much like I wasn't entirely satisfied with just listening to KISS, Sara didn't want to simply admire the work of IJM. She wanted to be in it. She wanted to be part of it. When she asked, "What can I do?" Gary didn't dive into the ways Sara could mobilize her tribe or the ways IJM could benefit from exposure on Sara's platform.

He said something more fundamental: "Become a person of justice."

What an answer! Now, I don't think he was just saying, "There are only certain kinds of people IJM wants in its ranks. If you're not that kind of person, we aren't interested." Instead, I think Gary had been around his work and the people who do it long enough to recognize and name what was actually happening in Sara. She didn't just want to do some good with her platform or tack on a charitable arm to her existing influence. What she had seen and heard about and through IJM had stirred in her a kind of dream or desire about who she wanted to be; she wanted to be someone who cares about, supports, and even does the work IJM does.

This is why it doesn't bother me much when celebrities or white suburban teenagers take selfies while doing charitable work; because somewhere in the noise of wanting to "look charitable" is the actual desire to be someone who does charitable things. Yes, there are miles of work between wanting to look the part and actually playing it, but I'm convinced there's a relationship between those two things.

Sometimes that relationship is dissociative. I might look up and realize I don't like the way I'm living or behaving. In other words, I don't want to be the kind of person who lives the way I'm living. It's not the behavior itself I don't want (overdrinking or being perpetually late to things or regularly telling half-truths); it's that I don't want to be the kind of person who does those things. Which is to say . . .

I don't just want to make better choices;

I want to be someone who makes better choices.

I don't want to just make good or great work;

I want to be someone who makes good or great work.

The ball game is never really what I'm doing, or even what I'm making;

the ball game is always who I am becoming.

I didn't just want to listen to KISS; I wanted to "get into" the music KISS made, even to the point of dressing up and pretending I was bassist Gene Simmons.

I really like what C. S. Lewis wrote about beauty in *The Weight of Glory*: "We do not want merely to *see* beauty, though, God knows, even that is bounty enough. We want something else which can hardly be put into words—to be united with the beauty we see, to pass into it, to receive it into ourselves, to bathe in it, to become part of it."[1] In the same way, I don't want to just hear stories about good neighbors and great works of love; I want to be part of those stores and live them myself! I want to be more than someone who appreciates life-changing work; I want to make work that enriches and deepens the lives of people who encounter it.

Now, I'm not suggesting you need to limit your interests. By all means, let your interests run wild and be as varied as the cereal aisle. What I'm suggesting is that you pay attention to those interests and discern the difference between them. There will be plenty of opportunities for you, and you get to do something for a short season out of pure interest and then put it down when things get boring or difficult. But near the core of our souls is the desire and *need* to do work we more fundamentally identify with: "I do this because it's who I am." Once in a while, we come across work in the world that calls on that part of us. In that moment, it's a tad more than just an interest; it's something more like a calling.

When Gary Haugen heard Sara talk about the way she'd been moved by news of the new abolitionist movement, he could tell something more than a passing interest was at hand.

Jesus didn't go to people and tell them he was going to do some really cool stuff later that day and that they should come watch. He said, "Come, follow me." He invited them to get in on what he was doing. And I think when he did that, he wasn't just trying to get folks to help him out. Jesus didn't ask anyone to be his caddy or Sherpa. I think he was doing what Gary did for my friend Sara. He was calling on that part of them that wanted to live fuller lives of loving neighbors and healing people and feeding the poor and sharing meals. He was inviting them into the active process of becoming. And the people he invited didn't stop at saying, "That's really inspiring that you asked me! How neat!" They got up and left what they were doing because something in them said, "Yes, I think I want that!"

Thank God that Chris invited me to not only listen to music on his stereo system but also be part of the 1979 East San Francisco Bay phenomenon known as Kid KISS. Giving in to that interest whet my appetite for more of the same. I liked being a conduit for other people's engagement with music. Later, that same interest in entertaining people blossomed into storytelling and jokes among friends, a habitual practice that made me slightly more enjoyable in social settings, even if it meant I got into trouble in classes. That day I got into trouble with Mr. Ross, who called on me in front of my speech class to take a real look at why it was I cracked jokes and told stories, gave me a first chance to figure out if it was all an insecure cry for attention or if these inclinations and interests in me were part of who I was becoming as a person.

Which is to say, in short, had I not worn makeup and rocked out with fake instruments in torn clothes while surrounded by several fire hazards the summer before first grade, I might never have become the author of this book.

What Do You Make of This?

1. What kind of work *actually* inspires you? (I'm not asking about what entertains you or distracts you.) What takes your breath away or gets you fired up? What makes you want to be a different or better person? Make a list of those things.
2. What do you think it says about you that you're moved by such work? What does it say about who you want to be or become?
3. What would it take to regularly expose yourself to that work? Instead of simply waiting for inspiring works to show up, what if you made a practice of that inspiration?

EIGHT

Loving Shakespeare

During my senior year at Clayton Valley High School, a local junior college hosted a showcase for high school theater programs. I was one of a select number of students sent by our theater coach, Tom Wills, to represent our school. The daylong festival featured mostly short, student-directed one-acts and solo performances. I was scheduled to present a monologue from our production of John Gneisenau Neihardt's *Black Elk Speaks*.

Walking to the middle of the stage, I waved to the small cluster of my friends sitting near the back of the auditorium. They waved back from seventeen rows away, even though there were plenty of empty seats closer to the front. Among that cluster of back-row friends was Jeff Hagerstrand, whom I've known since we were both two years old.

I felt pretty good about my monologue that morning and hoped Jeff, along with the others, felt the same about it. Jeff has always been a straight shooter when it came to pretty much anything in my life, including my stage performances. But when I found Jeff afterward, he was less interested in telling me about my posture, pacing, or diction and far more interested in telling me about what he'd overheard listening to the group of students from rival College Park High School sitting in front of them.

"Hey, isn't that the McRoberts guy from Clayton Valley?" one of them said.

Another replied, "Yeah. I've heard he's pretty good."

"Well, I hear he's a jerk."

"Yeah, I've heard that too."

I kept waiting for the part of the story in which Jeff defended my honor . . . but that never came. Instead, Jeff kept smiling at me and watching me squirm at not being liked. I hated not being liked.

The fourth or fifth time I heard Jeff tell that story (as I'm writing this, we're closing in on twenty-five or so times), he was telling it to Tom Wills, who chuckled, shook his head, and then promptly changed the subject. It wasn't quite the reaction Jeff was hoping for. But I wasn't entirely surprised.

Several months before the junior college showcase, Tom had sent me to the California Shakespeare competition to represent Clayton Valley High School.

"Wait," you might be asking, "Shakespeare as a competitive event?" Oh, yes! Think of it like a rap battle, but exclusively using verses someone wrote in the late 1500s primarily about the struggle and drama of life among the elite.

Each contestant was required to perform a short monologue and to recite, from memory, one of fifteen sonnets on the approved list. Perhaps due to the popularity of a recent film adaptation by Kenneth Branagh, a lot of students were choosing the prologue to *Henry V.* It's a wonderful speech. Upbeat, energetic, and chock-full of references to theater itself!

> O for a Muse of fire, that would ascend
> The brightest heaven of invention,
> A kingdom for a stage, princes to act
> And monarchs to behold the swelling scene![1]

So many students selected that prologue that my friends and I, a small group of students from Clayton Valley, made it a kind of running gag. As the first two rounds of performers took the stage and introduced themselves, they'd say something like, "Hi, I'm Tasha.

I'm from El Cerrito High School . . . ," and we'd whisper to one another, "I'll be performing the prologue to *Henry V*" and then giggle among ourselves. We were right about half the time.

I had chosen a piece from *Richard II*. The speech worked for me, not only because far fewer students had chosen it, which made me feel special, but also because the speech features words like *discontent* and *deformity*. I was listening to a lot of the Cure at the time, so performing Richard's character meant I could keep with the whole brooding, downer vibe.

Apparently, my plan worked. At the end of the first day, I was one of only seven finalists. Later, I noticed that four of those seven finalists were performing . . . (whisper it with me) . . . the prologue to *Henry V*.

During the finals, I was the fifth to perform. Before me, three of the first four had already performed the *Henry V* prologue. When my name was called, I walked to the center of the stage and said, "Hi. My name is Justin McRoberts. I'm from Clayton Valley High School, and I'll be performing the prologue to *Henry V*." Then, after pausing a moment to catch my friends giggling in the back of the room, I continued, "Actually, I'm not doing *Henry*. Everyone else seems to be." A few more giggles and sideways glances moved around the room, which was very satisfying. Finally, I introduced my selection, got into character, and put together what I believed at the time to be one of the best performances of my life—all 17.7 years of it.

I did not win the competition.

You probably saw that part coming.

The winning performer was an actor named Adrian. I don't remember what school he represented. I do remember that he had performed the prologue to *Henry V*.

Oh, yes.

Yes, he did.

It was a stunning performance, in all honesty. And I don't just say that for the sake of the story. The moment he finished, I rose to my feet and clapped, knowing, along with most people in the room, that he'd won. Adrian left the competition with a nice ribbon, a plaque with something written on it (in iambic pentameter, I assume), and a scholarship to NYU.

The following Monday, in drama class, Tom didn't mention the competition's results when he addressed us. He just said it was an enjoyable weekend and that he hoped undergrads considered attending the following year. When class was over, he gently pulled me aside and asked if I would find him at the end of the day but before rehearsal started.

When I returned to his classroom later that day, Tom

didn't even look up from the set piece he was assembling but said, "Your critique sheets are on my desk."

Flipping through them, I was honestly shocked to see how well I'd done.

"Wow! I scored 56 out of 60!"

There was a long pause before Tom responded, eyes still focused on his project. "Yup."

"Adrian must have scored pretty high then. Do you know what his score was?"

"Yes, I do. Adrian scored 58 out of 60."

"Wait, you mean I almost had it?!"

Tom finally set the prop down and walked across the room toward his desk. He picked the critique sheets back up and flipped through a few pages, then handed the packet to me and said, "I want you to look closely at the last line of the fourth judge's critique."

Beneath the notes about my projection, body language, and eye contact, there was a note written in large, red ink that simply stated, "3 point deduction for mouthing off."

I had won the competition, scoring 59 out of 60 possible points. But I'd lost because, as the students from College Park High School would note later that year, I had been a jerk.

From the time I enrolled in Tom's drama class sophomore year (thanks to the inspiration from Mr. Ross and his inflatable cactus) to my senior year, I would have said I loved theater. Acting meant I got to do something I was good at and that people could see me do it. I was liked, and I liked being liked. The first time I auditioned for a play, I was cast in a speaking role. The second time, I was cast as a lead. I could see where this was all headed: I would learn everything I could from Tom Wills and then go on to get a degree in stage mastery from the University of Theatrical Greatness (UTG), before becoming both famous and rich, eventually having Spielberg, Tarantino, and the Russo brothers added as favorites in my address book.

So, yeah, I *loved* theater!

Thing is, I mostly loved theater for the way it made me like myself. In other words, I liked who I was when I was acting, and I loved being celebrated. I liked the feeling of success, and I liked the public's perception of me. Now, while that's not the worst thing in the world, it's not love. I mean, maybe it's a kind of self-love. But it wasn't the kind of love I saw in Tom Wills.

His love for theater was at the heart of his decision to teach high school and spend countless hours in classrooms and rehearsals with kids whose commitment and talent levels could never live up to his own. It was also in the mix when he sent me to that competition. Obviously, Tom's kind of love for theater wasn't in the mix for me when I mouthed off in front of those judges.

Someone who actually *loved* theater wouldn't have been docked those points; they'd not have valued their individual performance over the beauty of the event and the art as a whole. Instead, someone who actually loved theater might have admired the work of other performers and celebrated their talent, maybe even been stunned at how remarkable a thing it was that so many people were memorizing such a great piece of Shakespeare's work as the prologue to *Henry V*.

But that wasn't my modus operandi; I was there to be seen and celebrated. I was there because I loved myself over and above the art I was practicing and the people with whom I got to practice it. Again, while being seen and celebrated isn't the worst motivation in the world, it isn't love.

In the Christian tradition, love comes in the shape of a cross. "This is how we know what love is," wrote the author of 1 John. "Jesus Christ laid down his life for us. And we ought to lay down our lives for our brothers and sisters" (3:16). Which is to say that self-sacrifice is definitive of real love. And yet, I think the way folks often think about sacrificial love gets twisted. In other words, I fear that folks sometimes read that Bible verse and think that if they enjoy something, they're supposed to "lay it down," meaning they should stop doing it and find something else to do they don't enjoy, as if doing something you love is sinful by nature because it feeds one's selfishness. And if the problem in the stories I just told you was that I loved theater, then my enjoyment of theater was inevitably corruptive; therefore, I needed to do away with anything I enjoyed doing if I wanted to avoid becoming selfish. Besides being bad theology, that's a terrible way to love my neighbor as I do myself.

The way I read this verse and understand the life of Jesus, I'm being asked to apply whatever skills and gifts and strengths I have for the enrichment of the world around me instead of the enrichment and celebration of my ego. In other words, instead of stopping stage work altogether when I figured out I liked it and was good at it, I needed to learn to offer my talents for the betterment of each play or competition I was in and whatever group of people I had the honor of performing for.

That's what Tom Wills was doing when he spent time with kids like me. Well beyond the class hours and the hours grading papers or looking at VHS tapes of midterm and final projects, Tom stayed long after class as well as after rehearsals. He worked diligently to develop the knowledge and skills necessary for great performances right along with a respect and a true love for theater. Which makes me realize that every time I stepped onstage during high school, I should have carried with me the honor of being a student of Tom Wills and a representative of his storied and beloved drama program at Clayton Valley High. Instead, I brought only my reputation—talent with a garbage attitude.

Tom passed away a few years ago. Cancer. My friend Jeff Hagerstrand helped organize the memorial service. His main contribution was organizing a performance by several of Tom's former students. As Tom had done more than two decades earlier, Jeff selected me, along with several others from various phases of Tom's career, to represent and honor Tom's storied and beloved drama program at Clayton Valley High School. Jeff divided up a familiar speech from Shakespeare's *As You Like It*, and a dozen or so of us read a short selection. It's likely you've heard someone at least make reference to the speech. It begins, "All the world's a stage . . ."

The character Jacques then goes on to describe the phases of life, from birth through childhood and youth and ultimately one's own death. Jeff had handed out our assigned lines a few days prior, which gave me time to think about how I would deliver my lines. Yet, as the morning approached, I was racked with nerves.

That is, until I ran into Tom's wife and kids in the

courtyard outside. Around them were a few students I'd acted with and several whose performances I'd seen since I graduated. Here was this whole world of people who loved this man in return for the love he'd given them as a husband, father, teacher, director, and coach.

We walked in together, and Jeff placed us all around the room for effect. As the opening lines of our monologue bounced around the architecture, I started remembering things Tom regularly told me about delivering lines of text. Honestly, it might have been the clearest I'd ever heard Tom's voice in my mind. "*Remember to breathe.*"

Then the first former student began . . .

> All the world's a stage,
> And all the men and women merely players;
> They have their exits and their entrances;
> And one man in his time plays many parts.[2]

Then Tom in my head again: "*Think about your character's audience. Not yours.*"

And then I heard . . .

> His acts being seven ages. At first the infant,
> Mewling and puking in the nurse's arms;
> And then the whining school-boy, with his satchel
> And shining morning face, creeping like snail

> Unwillingly to school. And then the lover,
> Sighing like furnace, with a woeful ballad
> Made to his mistress' eyebrow.[3]

Then Tom again: *"Don't choke the lines with your performance."*

And I heard someone else say . . .

> Then a soldier,
> Full of strange oaths, and bearded like the pard,
> Jealous in honour, sudden and quick in quarrel,
> Seeking the bubble reputation
> Even in the cannon's mouth. And then the justice,
> In fair round belly with good capon lin'd,
> With eyes severe and beard of formal cut,
> Full of wise saws and modern instances;
> And so he plays his part.[4]

And Tom again: *"Relax. Don't be in a hurry."*

Then another actor said . . .

> The sixth age shifts
> Into the lean and slipper'd pantaloon,
> With spectacles on nose and pouch on side;
> His youthful hose, well sav'd, a world too wide
> For his shrunk shank; and his big manly voice,

Turning again toward childish treble, pipes
And whistles in his sound.[5]

Finally, it was my turn. I found myself desperately wanting to avoid being noticed—a strange turn to take for a lifelong performer. I heard Tom again: *"Stand up straight and speak clearly."* And so I said . . .

Last scene of all,
That ends this strange eventful history,
Is second childishness and mere oblivion.[6]

I stepped back and heard a young voice from across the room: "Sans teeth, sans eyes, sans taste, sans everything."[7]

The room was still and silent for a long moment. Nobody was looking at me. Nobody was thinking about whether or not I'd done a good job—not even Jeff. Nobody in the room was thinking about me at all.

I really liked that feeling.

I might have even loved it.

The feeling of having been part of something beautiful.

Most of those in the room were either staring through the huge windows of the church building or down at the ground beneath their feet. And while I can't say for sure, I'd be willing to bet they were mostly thinking about either their own journey or about Tom

Wills, whose legacy was captured and embodied by that group of women and men, aged sixteen to forty-three, who had just recited a piece about the tragic reality that binds together most of the world's great art: life, after its many stages, eventually ends.

After light applause moved through the room and then faded, like a brief, soft rain, I realized that reciting Jacques's speech that morning, along with several CV drama alumni, had been the most satisfying and fulfilling "performance" of my life. I was part of Tom Wills's legacy as the director of the storied and beloved Clayton Valley High School drama program. I honored Tom by taking what he built into me seriously and making something beautiful with it, as opposed to taking his work for and in me for granted and just making myself look good. What a sacred space in which to give away some of the gifts and talents I'd been given.

What Do You Make of This?

1. What can you honestly say you love doing? Not just what makes you feel good, but what makes you feel like you're a part of something bigger than yourself?
2. When have your strengths and gifts and talents drowned out the voices of others in the places you've worked or served? In the future, which of your gifts and talents could you add to (not take over) a project that isn't yours?
3. Maybe you've been quiet too often when you should have spoken up about something you love doing. What is worth standing up for and being louder about? And how can you work with egotistical loudmouths like Adolescent McRoberts?

NINE

Follow Your Noes

Ever been the least cool person in the room? I have. Many, many times. It used to really bug me, to be honest. Not because I wanted to be cool, per se (although that's partially true as well), but because, when being cool is the currency, *not* being cool means I can't pay the door fee to the hip parties. Rejection, in any form, just doesn't feel very good. But, depending on what I do with them, rejection and denial can be essential elements of growth. It helps to hear the occasional no.

A few years into my music career, I was invited to join a panel of artists in the San Francisco Bay Area to talk about what it takes to make a living doing what we love. I was, without question, the least cool person on the panel. It wasn't even close. The panel was made up of

a graffiti artist (which is so cool),

a poet with exceedingly cool hair,

another even cooler poet with better hair who specialized in spoken word,

and a light painter (literally, this young woman painted using light).

Adding to the overall coolness of the event, it was held in the basement of an old leather workshop, which had been turned into a speakeasy. How cool is that? It's so cool! Twelve cool points out of a possible ten. I wore a T-shirt and jeans and introduced myself as a folk singer-songwriter and could feel the air leaving the room every time I did. It was like being the star of a reality show called *Lesser Than.*

The unofficial theme of the night was Rejection. Not because organizers had set it up that way but because the panel discussion kept gravitating toward stories in which artists had been overlooked, misunderstood, or flat-out rejected by the world of art and commerce: galleries that had turned them down, potential fans who didn't "get" what we were up to, and even friends or family who rarely asked about the work but regularly wondered aloud if we'd ever get "real jobs."

I told a pair of stories I hoped might get folks

laughing, since there hadn't been much laughter yet and because laughter is how I know people are having a good time. Neither story went over very well. In fact, immediately after I wrapped up the second story about a show of mine falling apart in Canada, one of the poets pushed back pretty hard against my humor, making the point that the difficulty of being an artist isn't a joking matter; that the world around creative careers isn't just difficult to navigate but actually malicious.

"I've submitted poems to the *Atlantic* more times than I can count. Every time, all I get is silence. They're not interested in real art from real artists."

There were nods and "mm-hmms" all around. Folks were really resonating.

"I mean, it's their loss, I guess, but it still sucks."

The light painter added her piece by critiquing the staleness of "Big Money Art."

"The downtown galleries are all the same," another artist said. "They're not paying attention to what's really happening out here on the streets."

Again, more nods and amen-like utterances of agreement and resonance.

And then it happened. I think it was inevitable, to be honest. But apparently the room wasn't quite prepared for it. An audience member who had been silent all evening raised her hand and said, "This question is for the poet in the middle. Have you considered that your poetry might not be good enough for the *Atlantic*? Have you ever asked why they don't like it?"

The room turned on that audience member quickly and with a vengeance. You probably saw that coming. Judging by the intensity of the stares and grumbling in the room, you'd think she had intentionally injured a puppy. Of course, she'd done nothing of the kind. She simply had the audacity to suggest that seeing one's work rejected or critiqued might mean more than "the world is a harsh place." Voices were raised, and fingers started wagging. Right before things tipped over into a full-blown shouting match, I picked up the microphone from my lap to say, "I honestly think it might be worth exploring the question a bit. I know I've learned a lot from conversations with people who didn't like my stuff."

And while I don't remember a lot of the details from the conversation that followed, I distinctly recall the general consensus being that even suggesting an artist's work may not be good is offensive (one participant called it an "act of violence") and that the main problem clearly lies with publications such as the *Atlantic* and the *New Yorker* along with most of the major galleries in the greater San Francisco Bay Area.

After the panel discussion, the evening was slated to end with a final round of performances by panel members; I played a song, the light painter showed some amazing slides, and both poets shared shorter pieces. Now, this isn't the part of the story in which I tell you how bad the art was by the poet whose frustrations and aspirations had set the conversation about rejection in motion. To the contrary, I liked her poems quite a bit. But it is worth noting that, even after hearing her talk about frustration with the curated world of poetry, the room didn't exactly rise to its feet, carry that poet into the streets, and parade her around town. Instead, I think audience members got to hear a very talented artist whose work was good but not great and would be better a few years from then (maybe fifteen?) if she chose to work at her craft.

And that has to be okay.

In fact, that has to be more than okay.

I should want that.

I should want to know where my limits are.

I should want to know *what* my limits are.

Rejection and being told no should be a welcome part of the process of life and business and ministry and art-making and growth of all kinds. Getting a no from someone rarely means the end of the road.

Getting a no can be a really good starting point.

Hearing no or being denied can be a tremendous gift. And not just the gift of developing resilient energy to fight through and prove everyone wrong, because not everyone who tells you no is wrong. Sometimes, a no means something else. Sometimes it means you found a limitation or an edge; and that might mean you have the blessed opportunity to focus on an area of work and life where you're better suited, better equipped, and more naturally talented. Wouldn't that be fantastic?

Most of the pressing questions artists, creators, and entrepreneurs face early on, as well as at various stages of their development, have to do with focus and identity: *Who am I? What am I best at? What should I quit?* In all honesty, the fastest route to getting these answers is by losing battles, being denied, and then exercising the discipline to figure out why something didn't work or wasn't received.

Of course, the other route is always available as well: the one in which I just blame the world around me for being so unkind. But that response screams of adolescent immaturity, doesn't it? "You just don't *understand*!" Maybe they do, though. Maybe you're not all that good at what you're doing *right now*, and that's what they're telling you. And if you were to follow a no every once in a while, the person offering it could help you. Sure, I'd prefer to learn all my lessons while winning all my battles. But there are unique gifts that often accompany a no.

Sometimes I wonder if I was taught to read *Romeo and Juliet* incorrectly. As I know the story, I feel like I'm supposed to think lowly of the overbearing adults who would deny these young lovers the permission required to foster their romance. Here's the thing, though: those overbearing adults were, in part, concerned that, should Romeo and Juliet start seeing each other, it might not end well.

Umm . . .

. . . well . . .

. . . Romeo and Juliet both end up dead.

It seems to me that many young artists, writers, ministers, and entrepreneurs live in a kind of Romeo and Juliet–inspired posture toward critics and marketplaces; they hear a no as a comprehensive dismissal and denial of their every intention and dream. As if Romeo and Juliet had been told, "You are not allowed to date anyone, ever, never ever ever," instead of "not that person and not right now." How would things have turned out for Romeo and Juliet had they learned *that* lesson? Heck, it's just as likely that over time and with a tad more maturity they'd have discovered they didn't really like each other that much!

One of the most formative and enjoyable books my wife and I read with our kids when they were very young is called *Art for Baby.* It didn't actually have much in the way of text. It was just black-and-white art pieces, a Murakami piece among them. My favorite page featured an untitled piece I eventually called "Negative Carrot." It was, in a sense, a carrot. But the artist hadn't drawn a carrot, per se. They'd blacked out all the space around the edges of the canvas until what was left *un*colored was the shape of a carrot. Sometimes, that's how I learn the shape of my work and life and relationships: by finding my limitations and endings and boundaries and edges. When enough of the space around the Real Thing is filled out, I can say, "Oh! That's a carrot!" Sometimes, instead of "it is what it is," I find out that "it is what it isn't."

That's what *no* does.

No forces creativity in a way a yes oftentimes squelches, pushing me to rethink things I figured were finished or apply myself that extra 10 percent when I'd actually settled for a second-best effort.

No pushes me to look for a way around, to find new angles from which to see my own work as well as new ways to make it. I get the chance to expand beyond my existing skill set and capacities.

No challenges me to look inward. What can I change, not only about the work, but how and why I make it?

No picks my head up to see myself in broader context. It might be that I started on a project because I needed to make it and that, upon completion, I find it just isn't helpful beyond what it does for me.

Sometimes it means discovering a new pathway, new audience, new purpose for the work I'm making. *No* can be formative. In fact, it often is, depending on what I make of it when I get it.

What Do You Make of This?

1. Recall a time when you received the beautiful gift of no. What did you learn from it?
2. Where are you hearing no right now? Have you asked the person giving it why you got it? What about you does that no call into question?
3. Where and why have you handed out a helpful no? Or where are you withholding a no that needs to be shared with someone close to you?

TEN

Tow Trucks, Trailers, and Best Final Shows

My very first musical tour was in 1999, with a band called Five Iron Frenzy, a punk/ska band from Denver, Colorado. At no point between then and now have I actually been punk or ska. So, for forty-eight shows, rooms full of kids who actually were punk/ska (many with dyed hair, Mohawks, piercings, and tattoos) were given the gift of a five-song acoustic folk set while waiting for the band they actually came to see.

It's worth noting that those forty-eight shows took place in just fifty-five days, covered ground from Bellingham, Washington, to Tampa, Florida, to Red

Hook, New York, to San Diego, California . . . and almost all of them took place in roller-skating rinks.

Roller.

Skating.

Rinks!

To be clear, I'm talking about rinks in which people would roller-skate.

It was called the Holy Roller Tour.

Part of what it meant to play that many shows in roller-skating rinks was that we not only had to travel with our own sound system but also with our own stage. Every afternoon, along with carrying speakers and cables and mic stands and instruments into the rink, we'd load in the roughly ninety pieces that made up the enormous wooden stage and assemble it from the ground up. Then some brave soul would test the stage by jumping on it. Once we'd established that the stage wasn't likely to collapse during the course of the night, we'd wire the stage for sound (cables, speakers, mics, drums . . .) and do the sound check.

On a normal tour, that'd be it. But this wasn't a normal tour. This was the Holy Roller Tour! So, after sound check, we'd detach all the wiring and clear the floor for the preshow meet-n-skate. A few hundred teenagers, who would pack the rink later that night and get teen-stink-sweaty while listening to their favorite band, would show up early, strap on skates, and roll around the rink, getting teen-stink-sweaty with their favorite band!

Then, once the preshow group skate was over, we'd rewire the stage, eat a few bites of dinner, and open the doors back up for the actual concert. *Then*, a few hours later, we'd unwire the stage, tear down the stage, load out the tech, and pack up to drive away.

But before we left, the headlining band would talk to any and all kids who stuck around after the show. This is the part that was most remarkable to me: that, after the drive (usually four or five hours) and the load-in and the stage setup (two to three hours), after the group skate (one hour) and then the show itself (two and a half hours), the band stuck around and talked until the last kid left. That's a heavy itinerary for even a few shows. This was forty-eight shows in fifty-five days:

Drive,
load in,
set up,
tear down,
skate,
set up,
play the show,
talk to kids,
tear down,

load out,

drive. . . .

Which leads me to the afternoon of show number 48.

The final show of the tour was Wednesday, November 17, in Dayton, Ohio, about six hours north of Paducah, Kentucky, where we had been the night before. The weather was beautiful, and our spirits were high. The finish line of this veritable marathon of a tour was in sight. We had begun reminiscing about the previous weeks and were joyfully careening up I-71 when we heard the sound of screaming teens. No, it wasn't the intensified echoes of our fresh reminiscence; the screaming was actually coming from the car next to us. The teenagers in the car were shouting and waving and pointing.

We waved back, thinking they were "fans" excited to see "the band" out in "the wild." They weren't. They had pulled up next to our tour bus to tell us that one of the wheels on our trailer had come off and that there was a hundred-foot-long rooster tail of sparks and gravel behind our vehicle. We pulled over to discover exactly what they had said (or rather, what they had screamed at us from across the highway while driving seventy miles per hour).

We hadn't blown a tire; the entire wheel was gone, leaving the axle exposed, which had carved a gash in the pavement extending who-knows-how-long up the interstate. In other words, just as that tower of flame and smoke in the book of Exodus led the Israelites through the desert to the promised land, our rooster tail of sparks and debris led this car of kids to some morons in a van.

While we waited on the side of the road for a tow truck to arrive, a highway patrol officer and his drug dog pulled up. The tour manager (his name was Clint; I believe it still is) shook the officer's hand and talked with him for a few minutes, showing him the wheel and laughing a bit. We'd been sprawled out, waiting along the side of the highway for about ninety minutes at that point, so we hoped highway patrol could help speed up our progress toward Dayton. He promised he'd get a tow truck to us ASAP and then asked if, while we waited, his dog could sniff around for a bit. "It's good practice for the dog," he said.

The dog lost it. Of course, you knew something like that was going to happen the minute I told you there was a drug dog in this story. Thing is, we most assuredly did *not* know that was going to happen. We sat in terrified shock, watching this animal snarling, barking, snapping, biting, and scratching at the back of the van. Eventually, not only were *we* sprawled out on the side of the highway, so was all our stuff. Bags and suitcases and backpacks and about half the contents of those bags strewn about the grass along the highway. The officer didn't find drugs of any kind. That was the good news. The bad news was that he did find a duffle bag full of cash. It was Clint's. As tour manager, he was responsible for counting, keeping, and depositing all the money from ticket sales each night. But because of the intensity of our itinerary over the past week or so, he hadn't been to the bank. Also, because this was before Square or any of the portable credit-card apps, the vast majority of folks paid cash for their tickets at the door.

Let's do the math, shall we?

$10–$15 per kid
× 800–1200 kids per night
× 9 shows since Clint made the last deposit
= A WHOLE LOT OF CASH IN A DUFFLE BAG

For the next hour we were cycled in and out of the highway patrol car and asked, one by one, to explain why we had so much cash and what we thought the dog could be freaking out about and what "ska" was. Eventually, the officer was satisfied that we were not running drugs between Kentucky and Ohio and made a call to have a tow truck help us get our busted trailer up the freeway. By the time we got the trailer loaded onto the tow truck, we were about five hours from our scheduled showtime and still a little over three and a half hours away. Of course, it wasn't just the drive that was going to be a problem; it was also the setup. While restuffing all our bags that the dog had gone through while sniffing for drugs, we resolved to make what we could out of our last show. We'd have to apologize for missing the group skate and start the show as soon as we got things up and running, even if it was going to be two hours late, which was very possible. We rearranged set lengths and decided which songs to cut from each set. It wasn't how we wanted our last show to go, but we hadn't counted on losing a wheel from our trailer!

We also didn't count on the police escort. Not only did a *huge* police tow truck lift the trailer onto its bed, but that truck drove eighty-five miles per hour straight to the venue while the highway patrol officer (whose dog hated our van) led the way.

We also didn't count on the small army of kids who'd arrived early for the show meeting us in the parking lot to help unload and set up. They had come expecting to join the preshow group skate. But instead of doing the crab walk or shooting the duck or playing a rollicking game of Red Light, Green Light with the band, they were now schlepping gear and lights and amps and pieces of stage from our broken-down trailer to the north end of the Fun World Skate Arena. Their help meant cutting our normal setup time by about two-thirds and starting the show only thirty minutes late instead of two hours late.

Lastly, and most surprising to me, we didn't count on that small army of helpers refusing free admission as a thanks for their help. As soon as things were set up, they walked back out and pulled sweaty money out of their pockets to pay the entrance fee, saying they just wanted to "support the band."

I've told that story for years now and even reminisced with some of the people I shared the day with. Almost every time, that's the part of the story we shake our heads at—that group of kids.

Trailers break down. Dogs have minds of their own. Punk/ska bands get mistaken for drug rings. These things happen. But it's not just any crowd of concertgoers who will line up in the parking lot (with smiles and willing hearts, no less) to unload and set up for a band that shows up late, then turn right back around and still pay to get into the show. And I don't think it's just that there's something magical about the youth of Ohio. I think it had a lot to do with what I'd seen during the forty-seven shows and fifty-four days leading up to that night. I think it had to do with the decision to not just book shows in regular venues but to do something special and memorable. I think it had to do with the fact that kids got half off their tickets if they came with cans of soup each promoter would then take to a local homeless shelter or food pantry. It wasn't the normal "bring a friend" schtick but "bring soup for folks who need help in your town."

More than any of that, though, I think it had to do with the way the band stuck around after every show. I was the most awkward fifteen-year-old anywhere between Bellingham, Washington, and Tampa, Florida, or between Red Hook, New York, and San Diego, California; I could wait until everyone else was gone and still talk to the goofy-cool trombone player who wrote songs about rhubarb pie and racism and kindness and grace.

The people in Dayton that night (and the kids we performed for pretty much every night of that tour) weren't simply entertained or even just inspired. I think they were loved, and I think they felt it. If Seth Godin is right that art is anything you and I make that helps forge a connection between people, then love is the primary characteristic of good art.

Is it interesting? That's good.

Is it well done? That's excellent.

Are people loved by you in and through it? That's art.

Good art sometimes looks like rock and roll and sometimes looks like spray paint and sometimes looks like sandwiches or tree houses, at least in its outwardly expressed form. But I think good art, in essence, looks like love and care and attention.

A few weeks earlier on that same tour, the lead singer of Five Iron Frenzy went home for a few days. A family member had passed away, and instead of canceling the three shows he'd miss, the band asked me how many of their songs I knew.

In Atlanta, Charlotte, and Nashville, I was the lead singer of a third-wave ska band. The set was shorter because I didn't know all the songs. The set was also different because I couldn't hit some of the notes. The stage performance was entirely different because Reese was a high-energy ska/punk singer and I was a folk musician. But what I still find most remarkable about those few days is not that this band asked me to fill in for their main guy or that they were willing to bend their set to meet my limited talent and memory. What I find truly remarkable is that not one person at any of those three shows asked for their money back. Not one. Instead, when I ran out of breath or couldn't remember lyrics, they'd jump in (with smiles and willing hearts, no less) and sing with the band they loved, the band they felt loved by.

I suppose it was not unlike the story I told you about that young performer at the fundraiser. Remember her?

She was so nervous people would hate her if she didn't perform well. But then she learned that people don't show up to see artists fail, especially artists they love! The Five Iron Frenzy fans in those skate rinks showed up because they wanted FIF to do well, and not even the absence of the band's beloved front man could dampen their enthusiasm. For those three shows, I was a member of a band that was sincerely valued and (yes, in fact) loved by the people they made music for because they sincerely valued and (yes, in fact) loved the people they made music for.

Was it interesting? Yes. And that was good.

Was it well done? Yes (even with me at the helm). And that was excellent.

Were people loved in and through it? Yes. And that made it art.

I've wanted to make art like that ever since.

What Do You Make of This?

1. What does it look like for your work to be an act of love—not sentimental feeling, but service and care and attention toward other humans?
2. What work have you done that did not communicate love? Why did that happen?
3. Where and when have you felt cared for because of the way someone did their job? What made you feel that way? How did it motivate you to do your work?

ELEVEN

Lacrosse, Bloody Noses, and Loving My Work

I didn't make a lot of friends in college. It wasn't so much that I was antisocial and busy during those four years; I just had a lot to do and didn't really like being around people all that much. One of the few comrades I had was Carrie. Carrie and I were in a pair of classes together, including a class I think may have been called "The Philosophy of Ethics in the Art of Modern Philosophy and Ethics." So, at least some of the time, we had conversations featuring names like Kierkegaard, Heidegger, and Nietzsche and talked about things like what "meaning" meant.

When we weren't pretending to be smarter than we were, Carrie and I also talked about lacrosse. She'd grown up on the East Coast, near Boston, and had come to California to play lacrosse for the Gaels of Saint Mary's. (Side note: I only learned after graduation that a "Gael" is a person of Scottish or Irish decent, making a Gael at Saint Mary's something like being "Irish" if you attended Notre Dame. For the duration of my time at Saint Mary's, I honestly believed our mascot was a stiff breeze.)

I'd only heard lacrosse talked about in jest and had never seen it played until Carrie invited me to catch a game. So after a series of clarifying conversations in which I learned that lacrosse isn't "soccer with sticks" or "grass hockey" or "a combination of both" as well as learning that if I "said that kind of thing again," I would "experience pain," I finally made my way to a lacrosse field, planted my feet right on the edge of the white line, and tried to find my friend. Between the quick pace of the game and the fact that the Saint Mary's players were all wearing white, I had a hard time spotting her at first. The Gael player who stood out to me wore a brownish-red mark on her shoulder, which I figured meant she was a captain. As it turns out, that player was my friend Carrie and that brownish-red mark was blood.

She spotted me during a break and bounded toward my spot on the sideline.

"Hey! I'm so glad you're here!"

"Carrie, you're bleeding . . ."

"I know. I got hit in the face!"

Up close, I could see dried blood on her cheek and jaw. I also noted the mark on her jersey was the size of my hand and looked like a map of Argentina. She spun her stick in the air and said, "I gotta get back out there. You should stay. If I can get a shot at the girl who hit me, you'll wanna see that!"

I couldn't help but wonder if, as much as she might love the sport, it was worth getting hit in the face for. She was bleeding, for goodness' sake! If it were me, I think I might have walked off at that point. But she smiled as she jogged backward a few steps from the sideline and continued, "You also might wanna back up a bit, so you don't get hurt!" I laughed until I realized I was standing there wearing a cardigan and holding a large volume of Sartre's *Being and Nothingness*. If ever there was a kid on the sideline just begging to become unwittingly involved, it was me. So even though Carrie thought lacrosse was worth a bloody nose and a trip to the cleaners, I didn't. I loved that cardigan and I'd spent over ten dollars on it!

In all fairness to the game of lacrosse, violence isn't actually in the rule book. Among positions like defenseman, midfielder, and goalkeeper you will not find "face puncher" in the mix. And while one of the positions is often referred to as an "attacker," I'm told that has more to do with trying to get the yellow ball into the goal and less to do with knocking someone's teeth out. Regardless, getting hurt is an expected and regular part of playing lacrosse. So, while "bleeding from the face" may not be featured in pregame strategic planning, Carrie knew that it's somewhat likely (if not *very* likely) she'd be hurt at some point while playing.

That's not just true of lacrosse; it's true of pretty much all athletics. In fact, it just might be true of life in general! Especially if I'm living my life with any kind of energy or risk or passion. Injuries can certainly be evidence of clumsiness. But at least as often, scars are marks of a life more fully lived.

For my part, I've sprained both my ankles multiple times, torn ligaments in my left and right knees, broken two ribs (both on the left side), torn stomach muscles, cracked my sternum, broken my collar bone (twice), separated my shoulder, fractured my left wrist (twice), broken fingers on my left hand, broken knuckles in both my hands, and cracked my skull (twice).

Which is to say, I've done some living, and I've got the scars to prove it.

Then there are the social, psychological, and emotional injuries I carry. These aren't quite as fun to list, even if they're at least as numerous. In other words, telling a story about dropping a portable basketball hoop on my head and being pinned to the sidewalk by the rim (happened in real life) is easier than talking about betrayal and insult and abandonment by people I trusted and loved and needed. Also, if I'm being honest, most of the social, psychological, and emotional injuries I've collected as an artist and pastor are deeper and have been harder to recover from than anything I ever suffered while mountain biking or playing football or dropping a portable basketball hoop on my head and being pinned to the sidewalk (yes, this was pretty traumatic). Also, once my physical injuries started piling up, I just stopped mountain biking (the technical kind, that is—rolling over rocks and boulders, dodging cows, other bikers, and the ground) because the thrill of the experience wasn't worth what it cost me in the long run. That is a *much* harder thing to do when it comes to relationships. It's easier to tell my biking friends I won't be taking those rocky, single-track trails with them anymore than it is to tell them I don't want to spend time with them at all because I end up hurt when I do.

Nonetheless, like physical injuries in sports, social, psychological, and emotional injuries are simply part of what it means to work in a field like artistry or vocational ministry (particularly the pastorate) or as a leader of any kind. But that might be where the comparison ends. My interpersonal injuries have been far more complex than my physical injuries. Not only because I don't always know how I ended up hurt, but because it is much easier to heal or even understand an injury when I've been able to associate an injury with a specific circumstance or person.

When it comes to emotional injury, I often don't know for weeks or months (or sometimes years!) that I was hurt at all, much less how deeply. Along with that, emotional injuries often come with a kind of shame factor that further slows, and sometimes debilitates, any kind of healing process. As a leader/pastor/minister/artist/public person, I generally don't feel like it's even okay to say, "I'm hurt." Admitting I've been injured is often interpreted as weakness or complaining. Sometimes (again, this has been particularly true of pastoral work) it is even considered an indication that I'm not strong enough to do the job or that I don't *really* want the job at all.

Some emotional/relational injuries have felt like soreness, the kind that comes with working hard and getting tired. But some of those injuries are far more like being hit in the face with a lacrosse stick. Many of those harder shots have come from walls I've hit while running full speed without paying attention. Others have been delivered by people who felt I deserved it and still others by folks who just seemed to enjoy taking shots at anyone trying to do something valuable or meaningful. Regardless of whether I was hurt by my own lack of wisdom or by the ill intent of another person, the effect has almost universally been the same: I end up wondering if what I'm doing is worth it.

What I saw in Carrie on the lacrosse field wasn't just toughness. I mean, sure, Carrie is one of the toughest people I've ever had the privilege of knowing. But *toughness* is just the word I use to talk about her willingness to endure the pain and injury that come with playing a game she loves playing. Which is to say, there's more to toughness than it simply being some quality we apply to everything we do. It's not that. If Carrie had gone bowling and ended up bleeding from her face, she'd have likely stopped midframe and gone home (probably to play lacrosse). But lacrosse and her enjoyment of the game were worth the pain.

Deciding whether something or someone is *worth* any pain endured is a question of vision and priority and discipline and, most of all, love. What I really saw on Carrie's face that day (along with coagulated blood) went way beyond toughness. I saw a love for the game of lacrosse.

Many, many (oh, man . . . so many) times in my vocational process, I've had to pause midstep to ask,

Do I love what I'm doing enough to keep doing it when I've been hurt?

Do I love it enough to learn to do it differently (maybe for the hundredth time)?

Do I love the people I do it with or for enough to take my injury seriously but not take it personally so that I don't become resentful?

Which brings me to Rickey Henderson.

Which you totally saw coming, right? (Okay, I'm sure you didn't.)

Rickey Henderson is one of the greatest baseball players to ever put on cleats. Because I'm an Oakland A's fan, I remember him as an Oakland Athletic. But the A's are only one of the many teams he played for over his career. After being drafted by Oakland in 1976 and playing there to start his career, he then played for the Yankees . . .

and then the A's again
and then the Blue Jays
and then the A's for a third time
and then the Padres
and then the Angels
and then the A's a fourth time!!!
and then the Mets
and then the Mariners
and then the Padres a second time

and then the Red Sox
and then finally the Dodgers.

Which is to say that, twelve times during his major league career, Rickey Henderson was traded or released to make room for another player who almost assuredly wasn't as good as he was. But as tough as it can be to get traded, that wasn't the real "lacrosse stick to the face" moment in Rickey Henderson's career. You see, the Los Angeles Dodgers wasn't the last team he played for. He would still end up playing for both the Newark Bears and the San Diego Surf Dawgs. And if you've never heard of those minor league teams, that's not surprising. Neither is still around.

Rickey Henderson, who holds Major League Baseball records for . . .

- most stolen bases in a single season (130),
- most stolen bases in a career (1,406),
- most games with a leadoff home run (81),
- most consecutive years with at least one home run (25), and
- most runs scored by a single player *in all of Major League Baseball* (2,295) . . .

played the last part of his Hall of Fame career in the minor leagues because major league teams didn't find him worth the money or the roster space.

But for Rickey, his love for baseball meant giving everything he had to the game, regardless of any circumstance, injury, or insult. Sure, he hoped to be picked up by a major league team again, but when that didn't happen, Rickey kept right on hitting and fielding and stealing bases and scoring runs. In fact, he played hard enough and well enough in those minor league years to earn All-Star MVP honors for one team and help the other to a league championship.

What I remember most clearly about that moment on the lacrosse field at Saint Mary's isn't the blood on Carrie's face and jersey; it was her joy while playing the game. Similarly, what I remember about Rickey Henderson's career isn't all the trades to other teams or even his final seasons in the minor leagues. I remember his drive and effort. I remember his love for the game of baseball.

I want to live my life like that. I want to do my work like that. So that the thing that shines clearest is the love in me for the work I do and the people I get to live with. The trick here is that the kind of love required in order to live that way is (like it or not) forged, tested, and refined in trial, including injury and insult.

While I wasn't traded or released twelve times like Rickey, and I never took a shot to the face like Carrie, the injuries, sadness, frustration, and disappointment

I've suffered as an artist and a pastor have left deep scars—and a few living wounds—in my psyche and my soul. At times, I still find myself limping to the sideline of my own life and having conversations with loved ones that sound like:

"Justin, you're bleeding. That looks like it hurts."

"Yeah, I'm not going to lie; it really does."

"What's your plan?"

At which point, I get to ask myself all over again,

Do I love what I'm doing enough to keep doing it when I've been hurt?

Do I love it enough to learn to do it differently (maybe for the hundredth time)?

Do I love people enough to be hurt by them but not let them define me—or not allow myself to define them because of the pain they've caused me?

Can I take my injury seriously but not personally so that I don't become resentful?

Do I have the practices and relationships in place to help hold me together and walk me through this?

Answering those questions isn't just a mental exercise for me; it has meant implementing and maintaining a specific set of practices that has led to a healthier work life as well as an overall healthier life.

First, I take therapy seriously. Athletes like Rickey and Carrie work with trainers, people who have studied the way healthy bodies are supposed to work. Those trainers have also seen enough injuries to help identify what's wrong with a body when it's not working well and offer help. Because my "playing field" is predominately mental/emotional, one of the most important "trainers" to have on my sideline is a good therapist. Someone who can see when I'm limping, when that "hitch in my giddy-up" has become so second nature that I don't notice it. Someone who can then help me feel normal because they've seen a lot of people with that same injury and can help me practice my way toward walking straight and upright.

Second, I regularly sit with a spiritual director. Rickey and Carrie worked with coaches who could see the game they were playing from a more comprehensive perspective. One of the ways I most often end up injured is by trying to do too much or cover too much ground. Instead of trusting in only what I can do well and wisely enough, I often try to play too many positions at the same time. A spiritual director helps me see my story in the context of the Grand Story.

Rickey Henderson played center field predominately, and my friend Carrie played mostly midfield-face-bleeder. They were responsible for their parts from play to play or from at bat to at bat. A coach, on the other hand, is looking at the whole field throughout the whole game and seeing each player in the context of a whole game, the whole season, and (if they're a more seasoned and loving coach) a whole career. A spiritual director helps me attend to the work and relationships in front of me; that's the job. Meanwhile, they help me see that my work and relationships are part of God's Cosmic Work, reconciling all things throughout all history in every square inch of history; and that's God's job. Sitting with a spiritual director helps me slow my pace and see myself in context.

It probably goes without saying that therapy and spiritual direction don't always keep me from getting injured; that's a pretty unreasonable expectation of either discipline as well as of life itself. But those practices have provided the wisdom and strength by which I've changed the way I live, and I have learned to avoid unnecessary hurt. More than that, I've come to honestly believe that an occasional stick-to-the-face is part of living life. That has meant I can take my injuries seriously without taking them personally. That same perspective has meant taking my work and relationships seriously without feeling overresponsible for every aspect of them.

Nowadays, when some loved one who can tell I'm hurt asks me, "What's your plan?" I know I have one already in place and at work. Which means I can more honestly and healthily reply, "I'm gonna get back out there."

What Do You Make of This?

1. What kinds of things in your past (relationships, work, faith) have been worth the pain? And what kinds of things have *not* been worth the pain?
2. Where are you experiencing that kind of pain now? What metrics are you using to decide if the project or relationship will be worth the struggle in the end?
3. What would it look like for you to take interpersonal or professional injuries seriously while *not* taking them personally?

TWELVE

Injuries and Great Audiences

I'd been asked to fill in for an injured player. Which is to say that someone had been hurt doing what I was being asked to do. That should have been warning enough. It was not. And that's how I ended up with this story. More precisely, that's also how I ended up with a broken shoulder, which is how I ended up with this story.

My wife played soccer throughout her youth, into her high school years and well into college. As an adult, she picked up playing again in the local rec league with a few friends. She is a talented player. So was the player

I was filling in for, who had been (important note here) injured while playing soccer.

On the other hand, *my* history with soccer is considerably different from my wife's. I played the sport for only three years, all of them before I was seven. I probably hadn't kicked a soccer ball in the twenty-three years between then and getting the call to take the place of a younger player who had been (let me remind you) injured while playing soccer.

Once on the field, I did my best to just stay out of the way. If the ball came to me, I pushed it in the direction of someone else on my team, figuring I'd either received the ball by accident or that I was in the wrong place and in the way of the ball reaching someone who knew what to do with it (ostensibly someone less likely to be injured while playing soccer).

And then it happened.

I was injured while playing soccer.

A teammate pushed the ball past me and shouted, "Go, J!" Sometimes, when I'm playing a sport or I'm with someone who doesn't have the time for all the syllables of my name (JUS-tin), I get called "J." This time, I'm assuming it was because the ball had been rolled past me on a trajectory that led directly to the other team's goal, which stood undefended about twenty feet away. I quickly formulated a plan to chase down the ball, lightly tap it with my foot, score a goal, and be carried off the field on the shoulders of my thankful teammates as they gleefully sang "We Are the Champions"!

There was only one player between me and Rec-League Soccer Glory.

As it turns out, one player was enough, and glory would never be mine.

I'm told I was in the air for a long moment.

I don't remember that.

I'm also told I was upside down for most of that long moment in the air.

I don't remember that either.

I do remember hitting the ground and feeling pain run from my shoulder, down my arm, and into my fingers.

I got up and continued to run around, holding my shoulder tight to my side, until the referee asked if I was hurt. "I think I am, yeah." Jogging to the sideline, I was passed by the young woman who would replace me. She has a name, but in the legends, she will only be known as "the Player Who Filled in for a Player Who Was Hurt While Filling in for Another Player Who Had Been Injured While Playing Soccer."

Once on the sideline, I was joined by Jesse, a good friend from church who had played on the team for the past year. When Jesse wasn't playing rec-league soccer, he worked in real estate, which apparently qualified him to diagnose my injury on sight.

"It's dislocated."

"Yeah, it might be."

"Want me to pull on it?"

"Wait . . . what? Why? No!"

At the hospital I was told I'd suffered a severe shoulder separation and that having Jesse pull on it would have been, in medical terminology, "a very, very bad idea and quite painful." I was also told to limit use of my left arm, which was going to be difficult since I was scheduled to be across the country in Philadelphia the next night playing a concert. I play guitar at these concerts, and that normally requires the use of both arms.

Much like the actual moment of injury on the field the night before, the next twenty-four hours remain hazy. I know I got from Oakland to Philadelphia, but I don't remember much else about the trip—only fragments and snapshots. In some of those fragments, my wife was saying, "Ooooh, I'm sorry!" as she drove our rental car over speed bumps. In another, I had apparently forgotten I was hurt and tried to pick up my suitcase. That fragment is actually pretty clear.

As the day progressed, my head cleared a bit. I remember sitting on the edge of the stage where I was scheduled to play that night, while Amy wrapped my shoulder with athletic tape. Our idea was that if we wound the tape tight enough, the separated bones would stay in place when I moved my hand up and down the neck of my guitar. Neither Amy nor I had asked the doctor about this procedure, but since Amy had been an art major with a minor in religion, and I was a performing singer-songwriter, we figured we were qualified to prescribe treatment for sports injuries. For the record, we never ran the idea by Jesse.

The show in Philly that night may as well have been sponsored by the makers of Vicodin. I don't remember all of it clearly, though I know it wasn't one of my best performances. In fact, one of the only clear memories I have of the night is one in which I forgot the lyrics to a song. It wasn't just any song either; it was a song I'd played in every show for the past year (probably seventy shows) and one that my fans definitely expected me to play. Yet there I was, staring at my feet while every single word of the second verse booked last-minute tickets to Venezuela and left town. I kept strumming and hoped the first words of the first line would come back to my mind (where they were born and belonged).

That didn't happen.

What did happen was probably better.

As folks began to recognize I'd forgotten my own song, they started singing the song for me. Not *with* me; *for* me. I kept strumming the chords, and the room picked up the lyrics. Just a few voices at first, but eventually the majority of the room was singing while I accompanied them. When the lyrics to the last verse and chorus came back to me, I joined them and we finished the song that way. Together.

I tried to clap with everyone else, but it hurt too much. So, as the room applauded, I just smiled and kept thanking them over and over. "Thank you. Thank you very much." I'd said it hundreds of times before. But this time, not only did I mean it a bit more deeply, but I realized what I should have meant every time I'd said it before.

The word *thank* comes from a Latin word meaning "think." The idea being that when someone gives you something or does something for you, you'd think about and remember the person on the other side of the gift rather than just the gift itself. For instance, let's say you gave me a cookie jar shaped like a dolphin that made dolphin sounds every time I opened the lid to get a cookie out of it. Every time I heard that horrid noise, I'd think about you (for better or worse). I'd remember that you cared enough about me to give me a cookie jar that prevented me from getting cookies in the middle of the night! *Thank you* can and should be more than a short phrase offered in exchange for the stuff people give other people; saying thank you can and should mean thinking of and remembering the people behind those gifts, be they cookie jars or shoulder wraps or the opportunity to play songs for a living.

And that really sank in during my Vicodin-sponsored moment in Philadelphia. I don't have *any* moments at all without the people in that room. I don't have a career without the people in that room!

Thank you.

I see you.

And I know I'm here because you've been good to me.

It turns out my lyrics and stories *didn't* just live in my mind; they lived in the minds and hearts of people who made my work part of their lives.

Listeners, readers, viewers—really, anyone who is enjoying art in some way—are more than just consumers of art; they're participants and cocreators. Which means that as I'm creating and building and planning, I ought to think of those folks; I ought to be working with a sincere thankfulness for them and the opportunity they give me. That means going well beyond wondering whether or not people will buy what I'm making when I'm done. It means asking a question a bit more like "How can people share in this?"

Too many sisters and brothers I know think and

dream and plan and build in isolation, focused primarily on how they can "sell" or "ship" what they're making once it's done. When the plan doesn't work out and pieces fall apart, so do they. I want to plan, create, and build the way Jesus did.

You've likely heard or read the story about Jesus feeding thousands with just five loaves of bread and two fish. There are two stories like that in the Bible, and they're usually titled things like "Jesus feeds the 4,000" or "Jesus feeds the 5,000." The way I read it, at least one of those should be called something different because Jesus doesn't seem to have actually fed anyone, not directly. Instead, he gave that job to the people with him.

Matthew and Luke tell me that, along with the twelve not-so-ready-and-willing men who actually handed out bread and fish to those thousands, there was a preteen with a sack lunch involved. Apparently, this kid not only got wise enough to pack a snack before he left the house to follow Jesus around the desert, but he was also kind enough to offer it when it appeared there wasn't food for everyone.

What I normally take away from that story is that Jesus took what that kid had on hand and did something truly remarkable with it. But can you imagine being that kid? Maybe you should! Because being that kid would mean, for the rest of your life, you got to tell your friends, "There was this one time when all these folks were super hungry and didn't come with anything to eat. So I grabbed the food I had on me, and Jesus and I took care of them. I'm so glad I was there! Who knows what would have happened if I hadn't come with my snacks!"

The folks at that Philly show got to tell their friends, "There was this one time the artist showed up on pain meds with a broken shoulder. We sang the lyrics he couldn't remember, and he joined in when he could." It's not the same thing, really. I know that. But it's not altogether dissimilar.

For Jesus, including others was a choice. Could he have fed thousands of people by his own hand out of thin air? My gut tells me he could have. After all, he not only walked on water and healed people but also kept the same twelve friends for three whole years! All of that seems miraculous to me. But Jesus didn't feed thousands on his own; he included a whole lot of people in that work. Just as Jesus does for you and me, he was drawing and inviting the people around him into the story he was living. We don't just have an amazing account of someone who does amazing things so that less-amazing people like you and me can watch him go while saying, "That's amazing! Nice job, amazing guy!" We get to share in and participate in and even contribute to that story, all the while thinking, *This is amazing!*

I was limited on the stage that night. I *needed* the people in that room. My limitations were a doorway through which others participated in and helped create a good, true, and beautiful moment. I think that's good art. I think that's good religion too. In fact, I think that's just good living!

What Do You Make of This?

1. Remember to *actually* thank people. Given the opportunity, take an extra moment to search your heart for the part this person played. Then, when you shake their hand or high-five them or whatever, look them in the eye and use the words *thank you* to let them know you see them; let them know they matter.
2. Create a list of people who, in the past month or two, made your personal and professional moments richer, easier, or even possible. Take your time. Maybe look through your text messages and calendar to remember. Let it sink in that you're surrounded by folks who are essential rather than circumstantial.
3. Then, looking into your next week or month, plan a way (dinner party? cards?) to let those folks know they're gifts to you.

THIRTEEN

Oh, Canada

The farthest north I've been without leaving the continent was on a trip to Edmonton, Alberta. Edmonton is roughly ten hours north of Butte, Montana, where I'd been the day before. Having originally planned to drive south out of Butte and head toward Twin Falls, Idaho, I'd been granted a last-minute opportunity to take a tour bus with another artist and play a few songs at a conference for Canadian youth. Now, ten hours is a long way to go to play three or four songs, but I was told there would be over ten thousand people in attendance. So I scrapped my plans to have a day off in Twin Falls and readied myself for the first step toward Canadian stardom.

You already know this story doesn't end with me successfully and flawlessly performing a four-song set to ten thousand new Canadian fans. So I'll jump right to telling you that the first sign my plans might unravel was when I was shaken awake in the middle of the night and told to get off the bus. It was just shy of thirty degrees outside, and a few ticks before 4:00 a.m. By all appearances, including the attire of the agents who greeted us as we stepped out of the bus, we'd been pulled over on a previously undiscovered ice planet northeast of Neptune. In actuality, we were at the Sweetgrass border crossing between Canada and Montana. Who knew Sweetgrass is directly southeast of Neptune!

I was wearing red plaid pajama bottoms and a worn-in T-shirt while I hurriedly rummaged through the storage bins underneath the bus. We'd been asked to unload all our music gear for inspection and then told to leave any sellable items at the border. That wasn't what I wanted to hear. My hope was that selling a few things would help me cover the cost of the trip. But even as I reluctantly handed over the boxes of CDs I had with me, I comforted myself with the vision of me trying to leave the stage while ten thousand Canadian youth chanted, "ONE MORE SONG!" (Which, you probably guessed, did *not* happen.)

A few hours later (and by "a few," I mean eight), we

were loading instruments into an ice arena in Edmonton. The conference director led us to the stage, where he introduced the headlining artist I was traveling with to the stage manager. They talked about set length and staging and lights and sound, and it all sounded glorious to me. What a moment this was going to be! But when I went to take my guitar out of the case, the stage manager set his hand on my shoulder and said, "Hey, brother. You're not playing on this stage. Your set is happening over there."

I followed the trajectory of his finger across the floor of the arena to a wooden platform roughly the size of a shoebox and situated *behind* the floor seats, facing a back corner of the arena. By the time I got my gear reorganized and across the floor, we had only about ten minutes before the doors opened to let kids in. That meant I needed to work my tail off to set up, plug in, do a sound check, and then find the emcee to be sure he knew my name. Since I'd been a late addition to the program, I didn't appear on any of the event literature. I didn't want to be called "Jason" or something! How embarrassing would that be! (Yes, that's foreshadowing.)

My sound check wasn't much of a check, to be honest. I wired my guitar to the direct input they handed me, and the sound tech told me he was getting a signal. I didn't get to hear what it sounded like to play on that huge system, parked about two hundred feet behind me.

"It'll be fine," he told me. "It's just gonna be really loud and you might get some feedback."

I was okay with loud. But here's the thing: one of the most reliable rules of stage performance is that, with very few exceptions, performers should just about never stand in front of the speakers while holding the microphone. What happens when we do is known as "feedback," which is a loop of sound information between audio input and audio output that builds on itself with increasing tension and volume until the system just plain freaks out and starts screaming, "This is wrong! This is all so wrong!"

So, as I was walking off, he shouted, "There'll also be a bit of a delay and maybe some echoing, so stay in front of the mic so the feedback doesn't get too bad." At which point he doubled down on his expectations for my set. "It'll be fine."

"Fine" is a pretty low bar. *That's okay*, I thought. *I'm going to be famous in Canada soon!*

As students darted around the room to find friends, pick seats, move seats, find more friends, and move seats again, I hurried to find one friend: the emcee. It took a few minutes, but I eventually spotted him as he was making his way to the main stage mic.

"Hey! Sorry to bug you. I just wanted to introduce myself."

"Oh, hi. It's Jason, right?"

"No . . . no, it's Justin. Justin McRoberts."

"Right. Okay. Roberts?"

"No, sir. McRoberts. With an *M*."

"Right."

It was already loud with kids running around and shouting over the video on the screen. The emcee (whose name, to be fair, I didn't catch) was thumbing through the program while we talked.

"Okay, here you are. Looks like you're not on for another ninety minutes. You're after the third speaker and right before the break."

"Great! Thank you. I'll be ready."

Eighty-five minutes later, I was strapping my guitar over my shoulders while the third speaker wrapped up her talk. She was shouting and jumping up and down while telling kids they were the future of their country. Kids were on their feet, clapping and hooting back. The room was buzzing as she walked off and handed her mic to the emcee.

"How great was that?!"

The room roared back.

"Well, there's more great stuff coming up, just *for you*!"

The room roared back again! I joined them this time. I was about to be part of that good stuff! I was there for these kids and ready to invest in the future of Canada!

"Ladies and gentlemen, we've got a very special musical guest for you this afternoon!"

Wow. What a generous thing to say! Especially since I was a last-minute addition. I mean, even if he was just setting me up well, that was very kind.

"She'll be on this very stage in just about twenty minutes!"

As people clapped and hollered back, it sank in that he said "she," which meant he wasn't talking about me at all. I was not the special musical guest. "She" was the far more popular artist they'd booked for this event initially, the one who suggested I tag along and got me this three- or four-song slot.

"So right now would be a great time to get up, stretch your legs, use the bathroom, and get a snack."

Oh, yes.

Yes, he did.

And as odd as it was when the cold, uninspiring houselights came on, and as chaotic as things got when the concrete walls of the arena started echoing with the buzz and click and clamor of ten thousand teenagers climbing out of their seats, the best moment of this story was about to happen.

I gripped the pick between my fingers and cleared my throat, hoping to capture as much of this moment as I could. Maybe if I opened with a strong enough few singing notes, a few students might stop to listen. That's when the emcee said, "During our break, enjoy a few songs from, uh . . . from Jason . . . um . . . from Jason!"

And there I was: Jason Um.

In front of me, on the floor of the arena, stood about twenty teenagers who apparently didn't need to stretch their legs and had brought their own snacks.

I had traveled to Edmonton, Alberta, hoping for ten thousand listeners.

I was literally looking at 0.2 percent of that number.

And I wish I could say that's where the comical nightmare ended.

But I can't.

Remember when I told you I hadn't had much of a sound check? That's usually not a big deal . . . unless you're playing in a huge ice arena and standing two hundred feet in front of the massive speakers. Just as the sound tech had warned me, there was a delay between my guitar strum and hearing it come from behind. But I had no idea how loud it would be.

IT. WAS. SO. LOUD!

I heard each lyric I sang and each stroke of my guitar *twice*; once as I actually did it at a reasonable volume and then again a fraction of a second later at full-arena-rock volume. The experience is pretty hard to describe. Here is what may be a close approximation:

Have you ever had someone mimic or repeat everything you say or do immediately after you do it? That's really annoying, isn't it? Now, imagine that person is actually you, mocking you, from two hundred feet away, through massive speakers in an ice arena while twenty Canadian teenagers look on, wincing.

I was in the middle of my second song when I admitted to myself that I was entirely miserable. More importantly, I could tell the twenty kids who'd graciously stuck around were something like miserable too. Between the double dose of Jason Um at two different volumes and the surrounding chaos of conversations and plastic arena chairs squeaking, there wasn't much good happening. Nobody was being served.

I can't say for sure exactly why I did what I did next. I'd like to think it was inspired wisdom, but I'm also fairly certain I was just fed up and it was a kind of freak-out moment. Before I played my third (and, mercifully, last) song, I yanked the chord out of the back of my guitar and climbed down from the shoebox-sized stage to stand closer to and join that group of young women and men without a mic or speakers—just me and the guitar and, well, one more song.

"Hi. I'm Justin." A few of the students said hi back. A few cracked smiles.

"Thank you for sticking around. I'm going to play one more song."

It was definitely awkward. But no more awkward than playing music for a half-dozen kids on speakers designed to deafen the hard of hearing from ten blocks away. I hadn't felt capable of making something "better" out of my circumstances. So I changed my circumstances and made something smaller. Turns out I made something more human. I removed myself from all the bells and whistles and took into my hands elements I knew I could make something with, even if it wasn't a step toward Canadian folk-rock fame.

Once I strummed the last chord, I said thank you one last time, pulled the guitar strap over my head, and walked over to that group of kids to shake hands and chat. I know people joke about how nice Canadians are, but this really was a delightful group. Eventually, the room was buzzing again from the reentry of the other 9,980 kids I thought I'd make fans out of. So I grabbed my guitar case and backpack and headed back to the bus, a smile on my face from ear to ear. No joke—I was actually happy with how that turned out.

Over a decade later, I got an email from a pastor in Canada. It was a really kind email, top to bottom, beginning with a few words about a recent blog post

I'd written. He then told me he had been among those twenty kids who got stuck watching my awkward set in Edmonton. "I couldn't believe you stuck it out," he wrote, "but I never forgot it."

He went on to briefly describe the circumstances of his most recent job as a pastor. He wrote about the dreams he had going in and the expectations his congregation had for him, just about all of which were disappointed within the first year.

> Nothing looked the way we thought it would and almost everything I tried didn't work. . . . Once in a while, I'd think about what you did. That you came off the stage and just played a song for us like we were your friends. I started spending more time with people one-on-one or at lunch instead of planning for Sundays, which weren't going well. We're way smaller now but we love each other, and I feel like I'm actually their pastor.

I know you're probably thinking this is where I'm going to say something about being "satisfied with changing one life" or "planting seeds." But you know that part, and you already came to that conclusion on your own. So I'm going to jump right over that and tell you about the *actual* takeaway from that story, the one

I've carried with me ever since. Yes, I liked that I set a positive example for that young pastor, but more than that, I really liked what I found out about me. I was so much happier on the floor with that small group of people, *actually* connecting through music. I was freer and more relaxed. I liked that I was willing to make the decision to cut my losses and do something that met the moment, and the actual people in that moment, instead of being committed to the expectations that might make the moment mean less. I liked that I was actually happy and that my happiness *completely* counter-balanced any sense of disappointment I had at not becoming famous (Christian-market folk-rock famous, that is) in Canada.

And here's why that's more important to me than even the wonderful story that young man passed along: it wasn't the first time circumstances had crumbled before my eyes or I'd been set up to look like a fool (a fool named "Jason Um," no less), and it wouldn't be the last. Not by a long shot. Things fall apart and go side-ways *regularly*. And part of what we figure out when that happens is who we actually are. Turns out, I was starting to like who I actually am.

You see, what that young man remembered wasn't just my adaptability or creativity; he remembered my character. And I really liked that the character he saw in me was real, that I wasn't faking it. He saw me floundering and struggling, then saw me up close, heard me without the tech and the lights, shook my hand, and talked to me like a human being. And years later he remembered it and believed it enough to try it for himself. That made me more confident that, whatever I did for the rest of my life, I could be surer that I was passing on something real to the people who encountered me in and through it.

Like it or not, you are the gift you are always giving in and through the things you make and do. That will forever be true, and there is nothing you can do about it. On the other hand, there is plenty you can do about who you are and who you'd like to become. So, when things go sideways (because they will, beloved; over and over, things will fall apart), you'll get the chance to find out who you really are. I pray you fall in love with that person and believe you're worth passing on. And may *that*, more than any set of circumstances or glorious setup, grant you confidence and assurance to adapt and create and reinvent and rethink and tear down and build back up.

No, that won't work for everyone. But if it works for you, it'll work for the people God wants to give you to. And that will *always* be enough. For instance, the organizers of the event in Edmonton thought it was really weird that I unplugged and climbed off the stage. I didn't leave a very good impression and was never invited back to that thing again. Then again, maybe they tried but couldn't find "Jason Um" on Facebook.

What Do You Make of This?

1. What big plans and dreams do you have? And what do those big plans and dreams actually say about who you are now and who you will be if they happen? What other paths can you take to get those same results and to become the person you want to be?
2. When have you been disappointed in the way something went? What do those feelings of disappointment tell you about the hopes and expectations you have for yourself?
3. When has personal happiness been part of your metric for success? What would your life look like if personal happiness was part of it more often?

FOURTEEN

Broken Bridges

The area around my house makes for some pretty decent jogging. We've got a good number of paths and parks, some shaded trails, and even the occasional drinking fountain along the way. I'm blessed to be able to leave my driveway, run four or five miles, and come right back to throw up on my own street. One of my favorite jogging loops takes me through Hidden Lakes Park, which is about a half mile from my driveway. The park features a four-hundred-meter track, a few playgrounds for kids, two baseball/softball fields, and a soccer field with artificial turf. It's a great place, as public parks go, but I specifically enjoy the network of trails *behind* the park. Those trails wind between a series of small ponds (people around here call them "lakes," hence the name of the park, but I personally think they're too small for "lake-hood"). Those ponds are connected by a small creek (as opposed to a river), which intersects the trail in several places. One of those crossings is particularly treacherous in the winter. Okay, by "treacherous" I mean that when the creek swells after we get a bit of rain, I find it considerably harder to jump across because I'm five foot six and don't jump very well.

For the first two winters I lived here, I'd get to that point in the trail and either turn around or plan to finish the run with cold, wet feet, which would mean not using those shoes the next day. Then, one winter day, I found a bridge had been built at that crossing.

Now, I'm not saying someone had pulled branches from trees and laid them across the water, haphazardly. Whoever this person was had hauled in pieces of treated wood (mainly two-by-fours and plywood), along with nails and a hammer, and they'd made a legitimate bridge, arching from one side of the creek to the other.

I stood on the structure for a moment and then did a thing you might expect from the average ten-year-old kid: I jumped up and down to test the strength of the bridge. Not only did I discover that it was a sound piece of guerrilla engineering work, I had a great time. Leaving the bridge, I raced home to tell Amy about it.

A few days later, we went on a jog together to see it, but it was gone.

You know those moments in movies when the main character discovers something that we all know is key to the story (a doorway or a body or a space-alien landing site), but when they finally convince their friends to go with them to see it . . . *it's not there?!* Usually, the main character says something like, "I swear it was *right* here!"

Well, that was me!

"Amy, I swear there was a bridge here. I was just here, and I saw it with my own eyes!"

We soon figured out what had happened. The bridge hadn't disappeared in some strange twist of sci-fi story-telling. It was far sadder and more disappointing than a space-alien intervention or a CIA plot to keep the feet of jogging people cold and wet. Just as someone had committed time and energy to building the bridge, someone *else* had committed time and energy to tearing it to pieces. There were wood shards along both sides of the creek and two-by-fours (with nails still protruding) scattered around the muddy, wooded trail that ran along the stream.

Amy asked, "Why would someone do that?" And I'll tell you the same thing I told her: "I don't know."

I really don't.

I don't know why we tear things down so often.

I don't know why we tear each other down.

I don't know why I so often undo good things . . .

in my life,

in my relationships,

and my soul.

I do know that it's always easier to disassemble than it is to assemble. It's easier to destroy than it is to put the broken pieces back together. It's easier to burn down than it is to form the ashes into something good.

The question of *why* we do horrible, destructive things to ourselves and to one another is one of the most complicated and difficult aspects of life. In the Christian tradition, we call this problem "sin."

Sin is introduced into the biblical narrative right at the beginning. In the third chapter of the first book of the Bible, actually. Chapters 1 and 2 are poetic and beautiful. Matter is created, along with space and time and light and animal life and then human life and . . . well, then there's chapter 3, where the serpent shows up and things go sideways.

A proposition is made,

a lie is told,

a deal is brokered,

blame is assigned,

shame slips onto the scene,

and it's all a horrible mess.

But among all those elements, here's the thing that bugs me most: the Bible doesn't quite let me in on where the serpent came from. It's just there at the beginning of chapter 3. No setup and no background. Chapter 2 ends with the words "no shame." Then, the very first words of chapter 3 are "Now the serpent . . ." I'd much rather have a way to make sense of the serpent's presence in the story, just like I'd much rather have a way to make sense of evil and the ill intentions in myself as well as in those around me.

As a comic-book reader, I really like origin stories. For instance, the Spider-Man story begins with a spider in a lab being radiated by some machinery, and then biting Peter Parker and *boom*—we've got Spider-Man. Or think about a young Bruce Wayne, who, after witnessing his parents being shot and killed by some thug in an alley, commits himself to avenging their deaths by fighting crime as Batman. Even with comic-book nemeses, pretty much everyone has some story about why they are the way they are and, therefore, what it might take to make things right. But in the biblical creation story, no origin story explains the existence of evil and the really hard parts of life. The serpent just shows up, and things go sideways from there. It's almost as if the writers and assemblers of Genesis were saying in their wisdom, "Hey, listen. This destructive, chaotic stuff is going to be here. It was here when we got here, too, and here's what we've figured out: Don't spend too much time wondering why it's here. Instead, watch what God does with it and learn to do the same. You're not here to figure everything out; you're here to make something better with what you find."

Which takes me back to that moment alongside the creek with Amy, staring at the shredded and broken pieces of wood and completely lacking a sufficient answer to her question: "Why would someone do that?"

I don't know.

I really don't.

And maybe there's something to that.

Maybe *understanding* evil and ill intent isn't my best road forward. In my personal history as an overthinker, too much time spent "figuring something out" has been a really poor substitute for "doing something about it."

Ben McBride is a friend of mine who works with lawmakers, law enforcement professionals, and citizens in an effort to fix the broken relationship between the criminal justice system as a whole and communities of color. He's a hero of mine as well. Ben doesn't spend a lot of time philosophizing; he's too busy planning and organizing and training and moving. Sure, he can talk all day about the history of systemic racism, the effects of redlining on black and brown families, and the disproportionate arrest and incarceration rates among black men under the age of thirty. He can also tell you about all the ways the transatlantic slave trade led to a utilitarian perception of black bodies and how that perception paved the way for a system of legal protections for white-owned properties that, passed down over hundreds of years, meant black Americans were treated not only differently under the law but as outliers to those laws and legal procedures. He's brilliant. He can do all that. But if you ask Ben to explain *why* it is, throughout history, people choose to create systems that oppress, degrade, and dehumanize other people, he'll just tell you that's what sin looks like. Then he'll tell you what he's doing about it and probably invite you to join him. If he does, you definitely should. Like I said, he's a hero of mine.

Ben's answer to the question "Why would someone do that?" is pretty much the same answer I get when I read the Bible. The Bible doesn't give me a list of ways to make sense of evil. What I get instead is a story about what God is willing to do about evil and even *with* evil. When I bring Jesus the injuries I've suffered at the hands of others or the ways I've been burdened, I don't get a lecture or an explanation or a philosophical framework. I get compassion. I get something more like "I'll share that pain with you" or "I'll bear that burden too." You might have heard a pastor, priest, or theologian talk about Jesus' response to sin and evil by saying, "He took it upon himself." I like that way of saying it. Which brings me back to that busted-up bridge and why what happened a few weeks later was so important.

After a good amount of rain, I turned the corner onto the path that led to the "treacherous" part of the trail. I was planning to turn around at the swollen creek and just head home. But as I got closer, I could see that someone had built a new bridge. (I'm assuming it was the same person, but who knows?)

New two-by-fours.

New plywood.

New nails.

It was a new bridge.

Well, not entirely new.

Once I was standing on it, I could see that about half of the bridge had been constructed using material the bridge builder had gathered from along the banks of the creek. Caked mud and water stains marked half of the new structure, as if to say, "I saw what you did. So I found the pieces you left and used them to make something else."

And this is where I'm supposed to end the story. Because this is the part that feels good. Also because all I've done so far is observe other forces at work and at odds. But that's not how life goes, beloved. And I'm not writing a book for observers of life. I'm writing a book for you so that you'll be encouraged to make something—even if it means getting ankle, knee, waist, and neck deep into the mess of it.

A few days later, the new bridge was gone. This time it wasn't torn apart in pieces. Instead, the entire thing was knocked over and dragged upstream about one hundred yards, where it was dumped on its side. Lying there, it created a kind of dam the creek water had to work around, which made the entire area a muddy, sloppy, swampy mess. I looked at the terrain between me and the bridge, and I took a deep breath.

You know those moments in movies when the main character looks into the dark cave or the haunted mansion or the disgusting swamp and then hears another character (who will probably die in the next scene) say, "You're not going to go in there, are you?!"

That was me. Except I was both the character staring at the disgusting swamp *and* the character questioning my next move. This time I didn't have anyone with me to philosophize with. All I had was a choice to make: What am I going to do about this?

It took me about an hour and a half to pull the whole thing back to where it had originally been and another fifteen minutes or so to set it back upright. I didn't get to finish the four-mile jog I'd planned to do that day, but I might have become the first #BridgeFit athlete in North America. I was soaking wet, caked in mud . . . and smiling from ear to ear. I couldn't wait to tell Amy to check it out. Which we did a few days later. And this time, when we went back out to the trail, the bridge was there. In fact, as of this writing the bridge is still there. I ran over it this morning. And as happens every time I take the three to five steps it takes to cross it, I experience the pride of knowing that, at least for now, I'd helped to beat back the looming and intimidating shadows that often attempt to turn us back from the path we're on.

I've come to believe that's all there is when it comes to sin and evil. I can't explain it away, and I don't think I'll ever chase it out of the world around me, much less out of my own soul. But what I *can* do is take a deep breath, stare the seemingly relentless tide of ruin and decay in the eyes, and say,

> You won't win.
> Not because I'm stronger than you,
> but because I'm more committed,
> more resilient.
> And you will not outlast me.
>
> If you tear it down,
> I'll just rebuild it.

I'll use what you leave behind
and add to it whatever I have.
I care more about what I make
and the people I'm making it for
than you care about tearing it down.

You will not outlast me.
When my strength runs out
and my legs are weak
and my hands don't work the way they
used to,
I hope and expect someone else—
who has seen the decisions I've made
and been inspired by the way I've lived—
will take my place.
You will not outlast us.

More than all of that,
I sincerely believe
the One who created all things
and who holds all things together
and is making all things new
(the same One who lives in me)
will do what was promised
and finish the good work begun
here in me,

through me,
and around me.
You will not outlast me.

Whether or not that sneaky bridge builder shares my Christian tradition, we do share something more than just the will and a way to cross a creek—we share in the spirit of creation and renewal. And I believe every time you and I choose to pick up whatever materials we have on hand to make a new thing, whether from scratch at the beginning of a project or in the aftermath of evil's best attempt at undoing our best efforts, we join in the long, unrelenting, and inevitable work of God to make all things new.

Every time.

We'll never create something that lasts longer than the Rocky Mountains.

We will never make something that cannot be broken.

But when you and I choose to create and then rebuild and then rebuild again and then restore, you and I share in the cosmic story of creation and redemption, a story woven together and eventually completed by One whose work lasts forever.

What Do You Make of This?

1. Can you think of a time when something you made or something you loved was destroyed? What happened? How did that make you feel?
2. What things in your life need to be rebuilt? What about something you rebuilt once but needs to be rebuilt again?
3. Do you believe things will ultimately turn out well? Why or why not? If you believed things would turn out well, how might that affect your work?

A Final Word

Just like there was no *David* until Michelangelo used the hammer to chisel that block of marble down and make it, and just like there was no hammer until someone strapped a rock to a stick, the fruit of your life is largely up to you. Yes, I think God does good things in and through peoples' lives, but I've pretty much never seen that work without the participation of the person God chose.

All of which is to say, I really do believe the future depends on you and what you make out of what you're given. I think households become homes because of your love and attention, that businesses and churches become movements with your energy and your talents. I believe, wholeheartedly, that applied energy and focus can literally set, correct, and reset the trajectory of another human life.

Since 1993, when I started intentionally working in the fields of art and religion, the question "What comes next?" has been a constant source of either thrill or anxiety. The thing is, most of the time I hear that question addressed, the answers sound as if some "next" thing is going to fall out of the sky and we're all going to have to readjust when it shows up. Meanwhile, the real "answer" to that question is being addressed by the courageous and resilient women and men who are (often very quietly) building it instead of waiting for it.

I didn't write this book because, after all these years, I finally and magically figured out what "next" is. I think *you're what's next*, and I wrote this book to help you become every inch the person you can be now that it's your turn.

I hope that as I told a few of my stories, you remembered a few people in your life who held similar roles for you as people like Tom Wills, Mr. Ross, and Frank Tate played in my life.

That story that changed your life?

That blog entry that woke you up?

That meal that seemed to stop time while you ate it?

That household you wished was yours?

That character whose journey was your journey?

None of that sprung from nothingness. All of those good works were created, refined, edited, remixed, stirred, and served by human hands who took a risk to believe that it was their turn, even if for just that day or hour or moment. But that effort moved you and changed you, becoming part of who you are now. See, while you were born in certain places into certain circumstances with certain parents and obstacles and opportunities, you will not be remembered for where you were born or what was given to you or even what was taken away. You will be remembered for what you did with what you had.

It is no mystery that the traditional, institutional places to which women and men used to gather with one another and with God to reflect on who we were becoming and what God might be up to are continuing to disintegrate, either by dwindling budgets or because they've simply lost public trust. In that light, I believe it will only become more vital that you and I take our creative and imaginative capacities seriously.

You're what's next.

Get ready for that.

Additionally, as someone who has spent his adult life thus far focused on the way art and religion bind people together, enriching the overall human experience and undergirding our lives with meaning, I think the future of meaningful life together is going to be smaller and more interpersonal. I think our circles of trust will be tighter and that *if* your friends, neighbors, and loved ones have a space in which they feel like they belong and find meaning and direction and purpose and hope, it will be because someone they know—probably someone they know face-to-face—created it for them.

I think you're what's next.

Get ready for that.

Acknowledgments

Amy—You make everything better, including me.

Mom—The best of who I am looks like you.

Monica—Your wisdom is a regular source of light.

Frank Tate—All my best decisions feel like things you'd tell me to do.

Dan Portnoy—I've never had a better friend or more helpful partner.

The Shelter-Vineyard Family—You've made "home" mean something real.

Donna Hatasaki and the Good Way Team—It is an utter gift to be arm in arm with you.

Tara Owens and the Anam Cara Community—There are things I heard in my own life that would not have made this book without your guidance.

W Publishing—Thank you for taking a shot on me. Let's help some folks make great things from what they've been given.

Notes

Chapter 1: Mr. Ross Sets the Tone

1. "Global WASH Fast Facts," Centers for Disease Control, April 11, 2016, https://www.cdc.gov/healthywater/global/wash_statistics.html.
2. "Report to the United Nations on Racial Disparities in the US Criminal Justice System," The Sentencing Project, April 19, 2018, https://www.sentencingproject.org/publications/un-report-on-racial-disparities.
3. "Poverty," World Bank, October 7, 2020, https://www.worldbank.org/en/topic/poverty/overview.

Chapter 3: Missing LEGOs

1. Voltaire, in *Oxford Essential Quotations*, 5th ed., ed. Susan Ratcliffe (Oxford University Press, 2017), https://www.oxfordreference.com/view/10.1093/acref/9780191843730.001.0001/q-oro-ed5-00011218.

Chapter 7: KISS Army and Becoming Something Beautiful

1. C. S. Lewis, *The Weight of Glory* (1949; New York: HarperCollins, 1980), 42.

Chapter 8: Loving Shakespeare

1. William Shakespeare, *Henry V*, act 1, prologue.
2. Shakespeare, *As You Like It*, act 2, scene 7.
3. Shakespeare, *As You Like It*, act 2, scene 7.
4. Shakespeare, *As You Like It*, act 2, scene 7.
5. Shakespeare, *As You Like It*, act 2, scene 7.
6. Shakespeare, *As You Like It*, act 2, scene 7.
7. Shakespeare, *As You Like It*, act 2, scene 7.

I'd Like to Help

If you'd like further help or guidance or encouragement as you take your next steps, contact me. As much as I love writing, my favorite way to pass on what I've learned is to do so directly. Let's set up a time for you to tell me what you're up to, what you're dreaming of, and what you're afraid of. I'd like the chance to help you make something with what you've been given.

justinmcroberts.com/coaching

About the Author

Justin McRoberts lives in Martinez, California, with his wife, Amy; his son, Asa; and his daughter, Katelyn. He spends a lot of his time coaching artists, ministers, and leaders and is also the host of the @ *Sea* podcast.

Other Books by Justin McRoberts

As people of faith, we all struggle at times to sustain a flourishing prayer life—a loss felt all the more keenly in times of confusion, political turbulence, and global calamity. *May It Be So* offers a timeless solution for the spiritual and skeptical alike.

We pray because we are human, not because we are religious. Something in our nature points beyond itself, and something in us searches for and desires personal connection with God. *Prayer* is a simple yet profound guide to facilitate the instinctively human desire to pray.